THE COMMONWEALTH AND INTERNATIONAL LIBRARY
Joint Chairmen of the Honorary Editorial Advisory Board
SIR ROBERT ROBINSON, O.M., F.R.S., LONDON
DEAN ATHELSTAN SPILHAUS, MINNESOTA
Publisher: ROBERT MAXWELL, M.C., M.P.

INDUSTRIAL RELATIONS DIVISION
General Editor: W. MARSH

Industrial Relations in Construction

Industrial Relations in Construction

BY

W. S. HILTON, M.P.

*Parliamentary Private Secretary to the
Minister of Public Building and Works*

PERGAMON PRESS

LONDON · OXFORD · EDINBURGH · NEW YORK
TORONTO · SYDNEY · PARIS · BRAUNSCHWEIG

Pergamon Press Ltd., Headington Hill Hall, Oxford
4 & 5 Fitzroy Square, London W.1
Pergamon Press (Scotland) Ltd., 2 & 3 Teviot Place, Edinburgh 1
Pergamon Press Inc., 44–01 21st Street, Long Island City, New York 11101
Pergamon of Canada Ltd., 207 Queen's Quay West, Toronto 1
Pergamon Press (Aust.) Pty. Ltd., 19a Boundary Street, Rushcutters Bay,
N.S.W. 2011, Australia
Pergamon Press S.A.R.L., 24 rue des Écoles, Paris 5e
Vieweg & Sohn GmbH, Burgplatz 1, Braunschweig

Copyright © 1968, W. S. Hilton
First edition 1968
Library of Congress Catalog Card No. 68–31407

Printed in Great Britain by A. Wheaton & Co., Exeter

08 013039 9 (flexicover)
08 013040 2 (hard cover)

1560220

Contents

List of Tables		viii
List of Diagrams		ix
Preface		xi

Chapter 1	Development of the Industry	1
	Changes in the Forms of Employment	1
	The Two Agreements	3

Chapter 2	Complexities of Construction	8
	Industry of Paradox	8
	Employment of Personnel Staff	10
	The Building Process	13
	Appointment of Sub-contractors	14
	Casual Employment of Labour	17
	Value of Output per Operative	21
	The Happy-worker Theory	24
	Top of the Bankruptcy Tables	27

Chapter 3	History of the Unions	29
	A Vital Freedom	29
	Combinations Acts	33
	The First "National" Unions	35
	The Document	37
	Strike Control	40
	The Working Rules	42
	The Strike of 1924	45
	The "Birds of Passage"	48

Chapter 4	The National Federation of Building Trades Operatives	53
	The Most Effective Federation	53
	The Composite Section	56
	The Central Council	59
	The Annual Conference	61
	Administration of the NFBTO	63
	An Important Link	67
	A Major Paradox	70

Chapter 5   Growth of the Building Employer   74

             The Early Years   74
             A Stimulus to Building   77
             The Midlands Strike   82
             The Federation Strengthens   90

Chapter 6   The National Federation of
                Building Trade Employers   92

             The First Functions   92
             Council of the Federation   98
             The Executive Committee   99
             Income and Expenditure   102
             Assisting Industrial Development   105
             The Main Task   108

Chapter 7   National Joint Council for the
                Building Industry   110

             A Highly Centralized Machine   110
             Building Trades Parliament   113
             A Three-part Document   117
             Democratic Organization at All Levels   120
             Green Book Procedure   124
             A Quasi-judicial Atmosphere   129

Chapter 8   Civil Engineering   134

             The Scope of Civil Engineering   134
             Signatories to the Agreement   138
             The Working Rule Agreement   141
             Earnings Compared with Building   142
             "Environmental" Factor   147

Chapter 9   Wages and Conditions   149

             National Working Rules   149
             Earnings in Construction   150
             Basic Wage Rates   155
             Apprenticeship   157
             Wage Rates for Females   160
             Working Hours   160
             Holidays With Pay   165
             Sickness and Injury Pay   169
             Termination of Employment   170
             Guaranteed Time   172
             Union Stewards   174
             Labour-only Sub-contracting   176
             Industrialized Building   179
             Incentive Schemes   180

Chapter 10   Solving the Problems   182

             Cost of Bad Industrial Relations   182
             A Basic Weakness   184
             National Register of Builders   187
             Register of Operatives   190
             Pensions and Death Benefit   192
             Redundancy Payments   193
             Inclement Weather and Guaranteed Time   194

Appendix 1   List of Operations Included within the
             Scope of the Construction Industry   197

Appendix 2   Constitution, Rules and Regulations of
             the National Joint Council for the
             Building Industry   200

Appendix 3   Addresses of the Hon. Joint Secretaries
             of the Regional Councils of the
             NJCBI and their Areas of Jurisdiction   226

Appendix 4   Procedure under the Emergency Disputes
             Agreement   230

Bibliography   237

Index   239

List of Tables

1. Number of Operatives Employed by the Various Sectors of the Construction Industry   3

2. Number of Firms in Construction   9

3. Employment of Operatives According to Size of Firm   10

4. Unemployment in the Construction Industry   19

5. Private Construction. Value of Output and Operatives Employed in 1965   22

6. Bankruptcies   28

7. Number of Unions Affiliated to the NFBTO; the Membership on which They Affiliate to the NFBTO Contrasted with that on which They Affiliate to the Trades Union Congress   58

8. Total Membership Affiliated to the NFBTO Compared with Total Labour Force in the Construction Industry   71

9. Working Days Lost through Industrial Disputes, 1956–65   128

10. Average Weekly Earnings in Building and Civil Engineering   143

11. Earnings and Hours in Building and Civil Engineering   144

12. Hours Worked and Hourly Earnings   152

13. Hourly Wage Rates   155

List of Diagrams

1. Structure of Building Site Organization   16
2. A Typical Trade-union Structure   49
3. Structure of the National Federation of Building Trade Operatives   64
4. Organization of the National Federation of Building Trade Employers   95
5. National Joint Council for the Building Industry   122

Preface

A VERY high proportion of the supervisory and management staff in construction has come from the operatives' ranks. Those in the industry tend to take a pride in this fact.

Certainly it is an attractive feature of the industry that—more than most—it presents young apprentices with remarkable opportunities to progress their careers from operative to executive status. But this "home-grown" management policy also has its defects. The most serious is that, until recent years, training and experience for them have been almost entirely practical, with very few firms providing courses of theoretical study.

And where training courses of this kind have been gradually developed their emphasis has, perhaps inevitably, been on improving the technical and planning aspects of management. The concept of perfecting industrial relations as an aid to smooth and efficient production is only just gaining general recognition.

Because of this there is a lack of published material dealing with the subject. Students taking the various examinations find their greatest difficulty is obtaining works of reference relating to employer and union organizations, and on the operations of the various forms of joint machinery.

Yet a thorough understanding of the present situation is surely necessarily dependent on a study of the history and development of the organizations which brought it about. The fact that there are no published histories of some of the major bodies in the industry gives some idea of the difficulty facing students.

This book is therefore an attempt to provide the relevant information, and in a collective form, which covers the basic needs of those studying industrial relations in the construction industry. It should also prove useful to those in employer, union and professional organizations who are concerned with the day-to-day affairs of the industry.

For their assistance in helping me to decide what was the most essential material to include I am very grateful to the officers of the Institute of Building. In the actual writing of various chapters, especially those where little published material existed as a guide, I have had valuable help from various people in the industry. None of them is, however, committed to any view expressed therein.

In particular, the chapters dealing with the history of the employers, and the structure of the National Federation of Building Trade Employers, owe a great deal to the careful consideration and expert knowledge of F. Oliver Jayne and Gordon Rowlands, both senior officials of that Federation.

For the important chapter on the National Joint Council for the Building Industry I am grateful for the advice and guidance of the Clerk to the Council, Frank Beazley, whose knowledge of its operations is unrivalled.

I also express my gratitude to Mrs. B. Wilmer who, at very short notice, accepted responsibility for all the secretarial and typing work essential in preparing the book for publication.

January 1968   W. S. HILTON

CHAPTER 1

Development of the Industry

Changes in the Forms of Employment

"If today a competent member of the National Association of Operative Plasterers were to meet the ancient Egyptian worker who used those tools, he might not understand the language, but could work with him all day till sundown without suspecting that 4000 years lay between them."[1] It is over 40 years since Raymond Postgate thus tersely summarized his impression of some building techniques as having remained almost petrified throughout the ages, and even during the period when technical innovations and discoveries had radically altered the system of production in Britain and created an industrial revolution.

To some extent, Postgate and other authors who have pronounced similar judgements on the industry were right in assuming that certain craft techniques have remained almost unchanged throughout the centuries. Building still calls for the exercise of handcrafts similar to those which existed thousands of years ago. But this is only part of the general scene, and to accept it as indicative of the whole picture is to misconceive the industry as being reactionary and perhaps consciously resistant to change.

In fact a great many advances have taken place throughout the years, not only in the continual development of new techniques and materials but also in the increasing use of expensive mechanical equipment—especially by the larger firms. Extensive specialization on certain processes in an attempt to achieve greater

[1] R. Postgate, *The Builders' History*, 1923.

efficiency has also made an impact. And these technical and material changes have been matched by changes in the employment structure of the industry and in the relationships between employer and employee. All this has led to an increasing complexity in the industry's operations which make it almost incomprehensible to the layman, and a difficult subject of study for those examining its industrial relations.

During the past century there has been a growing diversity in the differing forms of employment open to building operatives. This contrasts very much with the position just over 100 years' ago when the typical employer was a master craftsman in masonry, painting, plastering or one of the other building crafts and who mainly employed men of his own craft. The client who wanted a building erected had to make individual contracts with each of these master craftsmen for their services. This was a cumbersome contractual procedure which, though it enabled the various master craftsmen to negotiate the best terms for their services, was not regarded with enthusiasm by the client. Obviously, it would be much simpler for him if one contract could be made with a main contractor able to supply all the necessary craftsmen, or who would make arrangements for sub-contractors for specialist services. It was to satisfy this growing desire by the client that the general building contractor came into existence and the number of master craftsmen gradually diminished.

During the present century the diversity in employment has been carried even further and many large firms, such as Imperial Chemical Industries, no longer ask private contractors to tender for all of their building work but themselves employ considerable "direct labour" forces of building operatives. This same situation exists in the publicly owned industries such as Gas, Electricity and British Railways.

Nor does public enterprise in building end there. Various government departments, such as the Ministry of Health, employ sizeable forces of operatives. Many local authorities throughout Britain also have their own direct labour sections. When one adds up the number of building operatives employed in all of these categories—private and public—it comes to well over 1½ million, as is shown by Table 1.[2]

TABLE 1. NUMBER OF OPERATIVES EMPLOYED BY THE VARIOUS SECTORS OF THE CONSTRUCTION INDUSTRY

Employment	No. of operatives
Private contracting	1,153,800
Local authorities	197,843
Ministries and public utilities	177,621
I.C.I., steel companies and other private firms	120,000
All categories	1,649,264

While it is relatively easy to show the main categories of employment for those 1,649,264 men it is an almost insuperable task to encompass, in one book, the various agreements governing their conditions of employment. Even in the smallest group, where it is estimated that 120,000 men are directly employed by private firms, each company negotiates its own agreement and these are sometimes very detailed and complex. The various government ministries and public utilities also have their separate agreements and employer/employee joint councils, as have the local authorities.

The Two Agreements

In this book, therefore, the subject of industrial relations and the agreements which apply is confined to the pattern existing in the private contracting sector. This is the one in which the greatest

[2] This table was compiled in a research document produced for the National Federation of Building Trades Operatives in 1965. The figure for operatives employed by private firms like ICI had to be estimated because no authoritative government statistics are available for this sector. The three other categories are based on figures supplied by the Ministry of Public Building and Works.

number of operatives[3] are engaged and which provides the greatest output of value in any year. Even confining the subject in this way does not completely simplify it. In fact, it immediately raises one of the knottiest problems confronting students of industrial relations in the industry. For, if the industry's Training Board covers the whole of what is commonly accepted as "construction" and the Ministry of Public Building and Works provides statistics on manpower, output and other matters strictly for the "construction industry", it still remains a fact that the industry is treated as having two distinct parts—building and civil engineering —where the machinery for regulating agreements between employers and unions is concerned. The building side is governed by the National Joint Council for the Building Industry (NJCBI), and for civil engineering we have the Civil Engineering Construction Conciliation Board for Great Britain (CECCB).

This situation does not, of course, meet with anything approaching universal approval and leads to a certain amount of conflict within the industry. Most of the craft unions, which form the backbone of the operatives' side of the NJCBI, argue that definitions between what is building as compared to civil engineering work are often arbitrary and that operatives themselves seldom note any difference when moving from site to site. These unions also claim that agreements reached for civil engineering usually follow the pattern laid down by the NJCBI. They feel that, at best, it is confusing to have two agreements for what is virtually one industry. At its worst it leads to inter-union conflict with those unions which are predominant on the CECCB and the net result is bad for the entire industry.[4]

Although the unions are the more vociferous in their arguments over the existence of the two agreements, there are also employers

[3] Throughout this book the word "operative" is used to denote craftsmen, semi-skilled men and labourers. The agreements dealt with are those relating only to these categories and do not cover administrative, professional, technical or clerical staffs.

[4] At various annual conferences of the National Federation of Building Trades Operatives majority votes have carried motions asking for the merging of the two agreements in the industry.

in the industry who feel that new techniques and systems of industrialized buildings are rapidly eroding some of the major constructional differences which may exist between the two sectors. On the other hand, those who support the need for the existence of the two agreements claim that there are works such as roadways, tunnels and docks which just cannot be classified as building and they obviously require special civil engineering techniques and agreements covering them.

When Sir Harold Emmerson was asked by the then Ministry of Works, in 1962, to make a survey of the problems in the construction industry he gave particular attention to this issue—which he knew was an extremely controversial one—and finally declared that:

> Although building and civil engineering are integrated for statistical purposes there are real differences between them, and it would not be to the advantage of either of them if they were to be treated as one entity. Building is essentially an assembly industry which is undergoing rapid changes with the development of prefabrication and new techniques of construction. Civil engineering contractors are engaged for the most part on large scale projects, usually with less intricate problems of organisation. There is naturally a good deal of common ground, but it is important that the interests and needs of the building industry should be clearly identified and not confused with those of the civil engineering industry.[5]

Since Sir Harold completed his survey a further step towards establishing building and civil engineering as distinct entities has been the creation of an economic development committee for each sector. An objective observer, however, might conclude that these two sectors of the construction industry have the same independence of each other as have Siamese twins.

Certainly there are projects which can be clearly defined as requiring mainly civil engineering as against building techniques. But in many instances the line is very arbitrarily drawn and, in fact, whether the building or the civil engineering agreement applies on some sites may sometimes depend upon the trial of union strength which takes place before work begins. That there

[5] Sir Harold Emmerson, *Survey of the Problems before the Construction Industries* (1962), p. 7.

are such challenges for supremacy obviously reveals that certain unions believe their influence on a construction project depends upon whether one agreement applies as compared with the other.

The older craft-based unions, with their membership mainly working within the construction industry, generally support the application of the NJCBI agreements to site operations. They believe that the National Working Rules which have evolved through this machinery are more extensive and offer greater protection to the worker, and that the unions themselves have more participation in control of the project because of the detailed national and regional machinery which the NJCBI has.

Civil engineering has a much simpler structure for regulating agreements and no regional joint machinery exists between employers and unions. The Working Rule Agreement of the CECCB is less detailed than that of the NJCBI and the main emphasis is on defining the widely differing rates of wages for operatives employed on a variety of work ranging from clay puddling to driving a climbing tower crane.

The unions which are most strongly represented on the Civil Engineering Conciliation Board are, therefore, those organizing labourers and the semi-skilled—notably the Transport and General Workers' Union and the General and Municipal Workers' Union. The exclusive domination of the Board by the general workers' unions was slightly diminished in July 1951, when the constitution of the CECCB was revised to: "include representatives of craftsmen employed in the Civil Engineering industry who would form an integral part of the Operatives' side of the Board and have a full voice in the determination of the wages, hours and working conditions of operatives employed in the Civil Engineering industry."[6]

The general workers' unions, however, still have a majority on the operatives' side of the CECCB and they emphasize that this is reasonable because civil engineering operations involve far larger numbers of semi-skilled men and labourers, and fewer craftsmen than one would find on a typical building site.

[6] *CECCB: Constitution of the Board*, p.1.

Whatever the arguments by either side, the fact remains that the two agreements do exist. This should be borne in mind when reading the next chapter dealing with the structure of the industry, especially as the statistics on manpower and output can only be given for "construction" as a whole and not analysed to show the number of firms, operatives or output specifically engaged on building as opposed to civil engineering.

CHAPTER 2

Complexities of Construction

Industry of Paradox

The construction industry is one of paradox. In an average year its output includes about half the fixed capital investment made in this country. It constructs vast building and civil engineering projects and employs more male labour than any other single industry in the country[1] and, though its product is usually thought of in terms of such things as houses, schools and hospitals, its operations cover the extremely wide variety of activities listed in Appendix 1. Yet no other major industry in Britain is more fragmented or diverse in its structure. Though it may be responsible for thousands of millions of pounds worth of work each year it is still easier to capitalize a building firm than almost any other and, therefore, a large number of extremely small firms exist. And while it is true that new techniques and materials are assisting in the drive to modernize site operations, it remains at least equally true that in its production processes the industry suffers more inherent disadvantages in modernization than any other.

The purpose of this chapter, however, is not to pursue all the problems from which the industry suffers, but to reveal those which particularly make it difficult to achieve effective and continuous industrial relations in any one establishment and throughout construction as a whole. The large number, and diverse

---

[1] The operatives employed in construction are nearly all males. A relatively small number of women are employed on craft or other processes, usually in factory-type conditions. The only women to be employed on-site, and even then mainly on the larger ones, are usually found staffing the canteens.

character, of firms in the industry is itself an indication of the problem. The latest count reveals well over 80,000 registered firms in construction.[2] Contrast this position with the large industrial organizations which are now publicly owned and under central direction, and the crystallization of capital and control which is also evident in private industries such as chemicals or motor-car production.

Table 2, showing the number of firms in construction according to the number of operatives employed, is compiled from statistics supplied by the Ministry of Public Building and Works. These statistics are the latest figures available.

TABLE 2. NUMBER OF FIRMS IN CONSTRUCTION

No. of operatives employed	No. of firms	% of total
None	22,672	27·09
1– 10	44,800	53·53
11– 50	12,911	15·42
51– 99	1,770	2·12
100–249	1,010	1·21
250 and over	533	0·63
Totals	83,696	100·00

Table 2 reveals the wide variation in the sizes of these firms and, by inference, that they greatly differ in their organizational and capital strength. Only 0·63 per cent of the total number of firms employ over 250 operatives. Yet this would be quite a modest-sized staff for a firm in the general manufacturing industry. At the other end of the scale we have over 27 per cent of the registered "firms" in which the principal is the sole worker and has no employees—the one-man business. If we add this group to the

[2] It should also be remembered that this number relates only to private contracting, with which we are dealing, and excludes the many establishments run by private industry and public authorities.

next in the table we find that over 80 per cent of all firms in the industry are in the range employing from none to 10 men.

Employment of Personnel Staff

Obviously the capacity of the vast number of small firms for mechanization and general development is very limited. Firms of this size are also unlikely to employ personnel or labour officers to specialize in industrial relations work. The argument on this point is, of course, that the one-man business has no industrial relations problem and the principal of a small firm is close enough to his operatives to need no professional intermediary.

This argument is often taken a stage further by claiming that, in any case, the great majority of operatives are employed by a relatively small number of big firms and these firms—which are more likely to need skilled personnel staffs—are also capable of providing them because they have greater resources. Neither of these propositions, however, is really supported by what factual evidence we have. In relation to distribution of manpower by size of firms, the statistics compiled by the Ministry of Public Building and Works gives us the position set out in Table 3.

TABLE 3. EMPLOYMENT OF OPERATIVES ACCORDING TO SIZE OF FIRM

Number of operatives employed	Total employed by the group (in thousands)	% of total
1– 10	162·5	14·41
11– 50	280·8	24·79
51– 99	122·5	10·76
100–249	152·9	13·75
250–499	107·5	9·53
500 and over	301·8	26·76
Totals	1,128·0	100·00

Far from the *great* majority of operatives being employed by relatively few big firms, Table 3 shows that 565,800—just over half of the total—are working for firms employing between 1–99 operatives. The largest firms, in the 500 men or over range, employ a total of 301,800 men or just under 27 per cent of the labour force. The majority of construction workers is therefore in the employment of firms which would be considered quite modest in size compared with establishments in other industries.

What about the proposition that these smaller firms have no need of staff specially skilled in industrial relations? This is certainly a debatable point but, even if we were to accept that it is true, it would be wrong to assume that all the larger firms have personnel staffs adequate to their needs. In fact this aspect of construction management is still very much in the primary stages of development. It could hardly be otherwise when the whole range of management techniques in the industry has been held up for critical inspection and found to be in need of urgent action to make them more efficient.[3]

The problem arises to a great extent because many of the large firms have developed gradually from smaller enterprises. Their expanding capacity and the use of more sophisticated building techniques has not been matched by similar developments on the management side. The point was put very succinctly by Peter Shepherd, Director of the Shepherd Group and a past president of the Institute of Builders, when he stated:

> We are making an attempt to swing over to a professional management and I use this in the context of professional as against amateur. Most of us were thrown in at the deep end, and we developed as best we could. It is possible to have a more systematic approach to management development and this is coming slowly but inevitably in Britain. The first step is to recognise that management is a subject worthy of consideration in its own right. Good management can increase labour output from 50 to 100 per cent. . . .[4]

---

[3] The many problems facing the industry in refining its management and communications techniques are dealt with in *Communications in the Building Industry*, a report arising from a pilot study by Gurth Higgin and Neil Jessop (Tavistock Publications, 25s.).

[4] From a report of the proceedings of the Irish National Building Conference, held in Dublin in December 1964.

This statement is particularly significant coming from such a man as Peter Shepherd. The Shepherd Group is one of the most efficient in the industry, comprises about fourteen specialist companies, and owes its origins to Frederick Shepherd who was born in 1854 at York. It is therefore a reasoned judgement on the present position from a man with great personal experience of the industry.

Of course it is true that most of the largest firms do employ one or more officers to deal with labour matters. It would be a mistake, however, to assume that their opportunities for using refined industrial relations techniques on building sites are the same as in the manufacturing industry. For there is a very great difference between manufacturing, especially by production-line methods, and the complexities existing in the construction industry. When one thinks of Vauxhall's at Luton, or Ford's at Dagenham, the conception is of two autonomous work places where the labour force is reasonably stable, the site of production unchanging, and of a situation in which a permanent industrial relations structure can be created. Contrast this with the construction industry. The problem is not simply that there are over 80,000 firms but that most of them at any one time are carrying out projects on a large number of sites often separated from each other by considerable distances and continually changing in their location.

In construction there may be anything up to one million different sites on each of which it is necessary to set up the production process. The labour relations staff of any large firm may have to deal with problems arising on a dozen or more locations and, in each one, there might be a different pattern of production with the chain of command and the make-up of the labour force often varying considerably.

A large housing scheme may be under way on one site under NJCBI agreements involving different techniques and a greater proportion of craftsmen, compared with another of the same company's sites where the project is one being carried out under the Civil Engineering Agreement. The permutations in the number of problems which can arise are obvious and, though union officials and labour officers are often criticized for adopting "rule of thumb" methods instead of applying copy-book procedures, playing the situation as it comes is often all they can do. The industry is too complex and variable to make anything else possible.

So far we have confined our study of the industry's problems to those arising from the existence of a large and diverse number of work places and the varied range of activities which might be taking place on them. This brief picture is, however, far from being a complete summary of the special problems it faces.

The Building Process

It is when we concentrate attention on the actual building process taking place on-site that we see the full extent of the complexities of the industry. A building site is unlike any other industrial place of production. A complicated series of operations has to be married to a flow of materials and labour, and often on sites which may themselves present special problems. Nor is the direct control over labour and production processes vested in a single management as would be the situation in a factory. There may be anything from one to a dozen or more autonomous building firms involved on one site, and they will take their place in the production queue to carry out work which has been sub-contracted to them. Their relationships with the main contractor can vary from one of amity to the extreme where a great deal of resentment exists.

To comprehend fully the problems of site management and industrial relations in construction it is essential to examine the basic factors involved in the commissioning and carrying out of a contract. A major project may start with the client (except in the case of "speculative" building) approaching an architect to discuss his requirements. The client may, for example, be a local authority wishing to undertake a large housing scheme. When agreement is reached between the client and architect on the nature of the scheme they then set in motion a number of processes. The one we are concerned with here is the selection of the main contractor. A suitable builder has to be found for the job and this may be done in various ways.

The local authority may well negotiate a contract with a particular firm, or it may invite a small number of selected builders to tender. On the other hand, it may put the job out to "open" tender and the builder submitting the lowest will usually be accepted for the job. The architect, who is after all ultimately responsible to the client for the building, may or may not have confidence in the builder with whom he now has to work. His relationships with him can vary from one of caution to outright suspicion; at worst they may be openly hostile. With a negotiated contract made in relation to a specific and reputable builder the architect may be confident that the project will be built to specification and that no jerry-building will take place. On the other hand, the "open" tendering system may lead to a contractor being appointed whom the architect thinks will need to be watched very carefully to ensure that work is carried out to the correct standard.

On a local authority site, in fact, a clerk of works is often employed to keep an eye on the quality of building on behalf of the architect and client. To the man accustomed to normal industrial practice this relationship between the architect, who designs and is responsible for the project, and the contractor carrying out the actual building seems to savour of lunacy rather than logic. Certainly the situation is far from ideal. In Sir Harold Emmerson's report on the construction industry (already referred to) he lays emphasis on this point of possible conflict, and comments: "In no other important industry is the responsibility for design so far removed from the responsibility for production."

Appointment of Sub-contractors

As the job proceeds it might be expected that this conflict would ease. It can, in fact, often become more acute. The appointment of sub-contractors is sometimes a matter for difference of opinion. (It should be understood that the main contractor, who has accepted responsibility to the architect for the erection of the whole building, invariably has to make contracts with other firms to supply specialist services on the job.) The main contractor perhaps employs his own bricklayers, carpenters and plasterers and other operatives considered as belonging to the primary trades, but he may find it more convenient to sub-contract electrical, painting, plumbing and other work of this kind to specialist firms. The number of sub-contractors necessary on any job will fluctuate according to the "direct labour" forces employed by the main contractor. (It has been claimed that some main contractors only have an administrative staff directly employed by them and sub-contract all of the building work.)

The main contractor has much the same relationship with his sub-contractors as exists between him and the architect. If the architect has to ensure that the main contractor carries out building work to the right standard, so the main contractor must ensure the work of the sub-contractor is performed adequately. He will also have to plan the job so that sub-contractors are able to commence their work on agreed dates and so that any necessary materials required are readily available. Many specialist sub-contractors, of course, supply their own materials but the main contractor frequently accepts this responsibility and he will supply all materials where the sub-contractor is of a labour-only type. Obviously the main contractor will think that the best course, considering his responsibilities, is that he should be able to choose all sub-contractors required—perhaps firms who have worked for him before—and that they should unquestioningly accept his authority and direction.

On this point the architect may demur. He also has had past experience of sub-contractors and the type and standard of work they can perform. It may be that he has particular confidence in the ability of a certain sub-contractor and therefore wishes him to provide his specialist services on the particular project which is now being undertaken. The result is that he may "nominate" certain sub-contractors within the main contract and this leaves the main contractor with no freedom of choice in the matter. The situation which then sometimes develops is that the architect-nominated sub-contractor tends, as is perhaps natural, to regard himself as having a direct and special relationship with the architect. He may well tend to resent the overall authority of the main contractor (see Fig. 1 showing pattern of organization just described).

The conditions which then develop on-site have often been likened to a jungle. Indeed, the average jungle may well be more orderly. At worst, site operations may be nothing less than

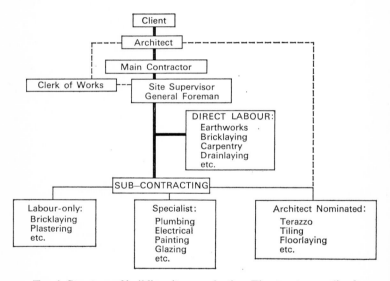

Fig. 1. Structure of building site organization. The structure outlined above has been simplified to bring out the textural points about sub-contracting and the relationship of the main contractor to the architect and the sub-contractors. The place of the other professions has therefore been omitted. The architect, for example, would have contact with other professions interested in the job such as the surveyor. The contractor also has his own professional and administrative staff some of which, like bonus and wages clerks, would actually be operating on the site.

anarchy. While it would be wrong to suggest that all building operations are conducted in such conditions the possibility of their developing is far from remote in some circumstances. Summing up their impression of this possibility, Gurth Higgin and Neil Jessop have written:

> At the present time the roles in the building industry are in a state of considerable confusion. The implications of this for the experience of any individual in the building team are, firstly, he finds that there is no settled and stable definition of what his job actually is, and secondly, nobody else can be clear about exactly what he does and what he is responsible for without finding out a lot more about the sort of building team he is in. The architect, the builder, the quantity surveyor, the sub-contractor, will be doing quite different jobs depending upon which of the many possible patterns of team structure they are currently operating in.[5]

These are certainly not circumstances which make it easy to implement a stable system of industrial relations which, after all, are based on sound personal links between management and representatives of the men. The very nature of the construction process implies a sporadic and casual relationship between the professions, the builder, sub-contractors and the operatives. Labour, in general, is hired for a specific job and fired at the end of it. This is not simply due to ruthlessness on the part of the employer. He may complete one job in Manchester and have to open up his next site in London and, even though building workers are the last of the race of industrial nomads prepared to accept a life of casual employment which most other workers would find unendurable, they will not wish to travel such a distance from home in order to maintain continuity of employment with one firm.

Casual Employment of Labour

By necessity, therefore, the contractor finds that apart from a few key staff who may remain more continually in his employment, he has to build up a fresh labour force for each major

[5] *Communications in the Building Industry*, p. 61.

project. Nor should it be assumed that such a labour force will remain stable even for the duration of a given project. Craftsmen will be brought on the site and leave when their particular part of the job is completed. Sub-contractors will move their men on and off according to the terms of their agreement with the main contractor. Operatives will also be sacked for one reason or other during the course of the job, or will leave of their own accord. The whole situation, therefore, is in a constant state of flux in which it is almost impossible to ensure that one experienced manager or labour officer will be able to maintain relationships throughout the length of the job with experienced union stewards representing the men.

In these circumstances the role of the labour officer and full-time union official is extremely difficult. It is almost impossible for them to establish on-site systems of industrial relations of such a positive nature that they can be relied upon to prevent trouble from arising. Their role, in fact, is generally to swing into action when trouble has already broken out and try to get it under control as soon as possible. They act as trouble shooters. They know that even if they were able to surmount some of the difficulties endemic in construction they would still be dependent on the weather for continuous site operations.

The adverse effects of inclement weather can vary between the stoppage of site work for an hour or two, because of heavy rain, and the extreme where a planned production schedule is completely disrupted due to severe and prolonged frost. The job may have been carefully programmed with its various phases reaching target dates; an experienced labour force may have reached optimum productivity—and then the sudden onset of bad weather completely closes down the site.

For the contractor this situation, over which he has no control, is disastrous to his plans. He loses production time. His phased building schedule is disorganized and the bulk of his labour force will probably have to be sent off to the employment exchange; perhaps when the thaw finally comes they will have drifted into other jobs. His painstaking efforts to build up a labour force must be gone through again. His job will have to be rephased and possibly new arrangements made with his sub-contractors, for the freeze-up will also have brought similar problems for them. It may be months before the job again reaches the optimum level of production.

Even in a relatively mild winter unemployment increases in construction. This is one of the facts of life in the industry which has become accepted by employers, clients and the operatives alike. It is also one of the reasons why, even apart from any stop–go economic crisis, the industry provides a high proportion of casual employment. Table 4 shows the variation which can take place between summer and winter unemployment in construction and relates to the period from January 1964 to July 1966.

TABLE 4. UNEMPLOYMENT IN THE CONSTRUCTION INDUSTRY*

Date	Craftsmen	Others	Total
1964 Jan.	16,123	56,321	72,444
July	6,225	34,139	40,364
1965 Jan.	12,609	43,303	55,912
July	5,804	30,507	36,311
1966 Jan.	15,813	39,341	55,154
July	7,731	27,201	34,932

* Figures taken from *Monthly Bulletin of Construction Statistics*, published by the Ministry of Public Building and Works.

In the years covered by Table 4 the winters were comparatively mild. The similarity of climatic conditions can be inferred from the column showing the level of unemployment among craftsmen, which is a rather more accurate indictor than the "Others" column which relates to labourers, semi-skilled and unclassified. These figures for craftsmen show little variation apart from the fact that general levels of unemployment in 1965 were rather less than in the other two years.

Averaging the figures out over the period from 1964 to 1966 we get an average of 37,202 operatives unemployed in July months as against 61,170 in January. Even in a normal year, therefore, winter unemployment is likely run at a level some 61 per cent above the summer total.

Apart from the insecurity and loss of earnings this means for the operatives, there is obviously an adverse effect on production generally in the construction industry. The impact of a really severe winter, however, is very much greater. The last one in this country occurred at the beginning of 1963. In February, at the time when the freeze-up was at its worst, unemployment rapidly rose to a total of 138,017—nearly $2\frac{1}{2}$ times above the average winter figure. Some jobs were stopped for many weeks and the total loss in output for the industry was estimated at around £100 million. It was some months before the industry again reached normal operational levels and, when it did so, it was without the assistance of many operatives who had left for good to go into manufacturing and other industries to secure more stable employment.

It is because bad weather aggravates all the problems which normally bedevil the industry that special attention has been paid to overcoming the worst effects of a bad winter. The Ministry of Public Building and Works has, in recent years, done a great deal to discover and popularize methods of working which help to beat the frost. These activities were stepped up after the freeze-up of 1963. If that winter can be deprecated because it held back production on the sites, at least it accelerated the appointment of the Ministry's first Winter Building Advisor!

The adverse impact of bad weather is revealed more dramatically on sites engaged in new work and, because of this, it has been suggested that one solution is that firms should diversify their activities so they can "fall back" on repairs and maintenance. This would then obviate the need to sack the bulk of their operatives. Obviously anything which can help maintain a balanced labour force in continuous employment is to be desired, but diversification of work in this way is easier to propose than to practise. Different techniques, and even a rather different class of operative, are required for new construction compared to repairs and maintenance. Nor is it practicable to move a few hundred men from a shut-down site, perhaps engaged on building a power station in a remote country area, and transport them to the nearest urban area to carry out repairs and maintenance work.

It is fallacious, in any case, to imply that repairs and mainten-ance is an area of activity which is itself free from interruption by inclement weather. Certainly constant frost stimulates the work of the plumber, but this is generally more than offset by the adverse effect on the painting trade and on other operatives engaged on outside repairs and maintenance. As a considerable proportion of men are employed in the repair and maintenance sector—323,000 or over 28 per cent of the total labour force in private construction—even if inclement weather throws only a small percentage of them out of work it can mean unemployment for some thousands of men.

Value of Output per Operative

Table 5, relating to the year 1965 (which was the post-war peak year for employment in the industry), underlines this point by showing the number of operatives employed on repairs and maintenance contrasted with those on new housing, industrial building and other work. It also gives the value of output in each of the sectors and this reveals another of the problems upon which attention is now being focused in the industry: the disparity in value of output per man between the various categories of work. For example, the total labour force of 319,000 operatives employed on new housing (local authority and private development) produced £3294 annual value of output per man compared with £2077 per man employed on repairs and maintenance.

TABLE 5. PRIVATE CONSTRUCTION. VALUE OF OUTPUT AND
OPERATIVES EMPLOYED IN 1965[6]

Class of work	Value in £ million	No. of operatives (in thousands)
New Housing		
For public authorities	466	149
For private developers	585	170
Other New Work		
For public authorities	739	213
For private developers:		
Industrial	433	128
Miscellaneous	408	143
Repair and Maintenance	671	323
Total: All work	3302	1126

The low value productivity per man in the repairs and maintenance sector has been critically examined in the industry with
a view to finding out what stimulus incentive-bonus schemes
might have. This line of inquiry has also been stimulated in the
Government's National Plan, produced in conjunction with the
economic and development committees for building and civil
engineering, which affirms that increasing demand on the industry
must be met by greater productivity rather than by proportion-
ately increasing the labour force.

The major difficulty in implementing bonus schemes for
repairs and maintenance is that a great deal of this work is non-
repetitive. It is therefore not easy to establish target output
figures. This is not, however, the sole reason why so little has
been done on this matter. Incentive schemes, if they are to be

[6] The table is based on statistics contained in the *Monthly Bulletin* published by the Ministry of Public Building and Works. It should be noted that
the figure for the total number of operatives of 1,126,000 is the average for
the whole year and therefore differs from that in Table 1, Chapter 1, which
shows the number employed in the month of April 1965.

sound and produce the desired results, should be based on accumulated work performance records and supervised by qualified staff. In other words, their existence is usually indicative of an efficient managerial system. And this is the point at which we return to the original criticisms about the present standard of management practice in the industry.

It would be reasonable to claim that the failure to implement incentives on a wider scale in construction generally is due more to managerial deficiencies than the problems endemic in the industry's operations. For though it is admittedly difficult to apply incentives to repairs and maintenance, it is relatively simple to establish targets for new building work. Yet it has been revealed that in the construction industry only about 17 per cent of the operatives carry out their work under genuine target-related incentive schemes, although about 70 per cent of the labour force is engaged on new work.[7] And this at a time when almost every other industry has accepted that, in a continuing situation of full employment, incentive schemes are essential tools for increasing productivity.

Of course it is known that a great part of the labour force in the construction industry receives wage rates which are well above those agreed by the national joint councils, but these are often in the form of straight plus-rates or other payments not directly related to measured output. It is regrettable that the industry has not yet, as a whole, become more clearly aware of the major significance of the introduction of soundly based incentives. These schemes should not be regarded simply as the alternative to which management feels reluctantly driven because the "whiplash of unemployment" no longer exists as the major stimulus to productivity. Reasonably targeted bonus schemes are, in effect, the hub around which greater site efficiency can develop and construction itself become less of a hit-and-miss affair.

[7] The Ministry of Labour conducts a periodical survey of payment by results in industry, and reports are published in the *Ministry of Labour Gazette*. The figure of 17 per cent in relation to the construction industry is the average over the past few years according to these surveys.

This point was made very emphatically in the report on "Organization of Building Sites" carried out by the Building Research Station where it was stated that firms employing such schemes had no doubt that: "Well-run systems of fairly direct output payments had been successful . . . in obtaining higher productivity and earnings, and shorter building time, than would otherwise have been possible. Furthermore, a well-established and fairly direct system can provide a useful interim guide, through the level of output payments earned, to the satisfactory progress and organization of a site."[8]

Another valid inference which can be made from this is that the contract upon which a good system of incentives has been evolved is also likely to have more amicable relations between management and men; for the attainment of efficiency through measured bonus schemes suggests a number of essential preconditions. One can assume that the site has been kept reasonably tidy and does not simulate the appearance of a junk-yard. Materials will be kept flowing on to the job in an orderly fashion as required, and stacked near at hand for the men using them. This means that impediments to production are reduced and the operative is able to work as fast, and earn as much, as his own personal inclinations dictate.

Seen in this light incentive schemes could be one of the major keys in opening the door to better industrial relations. For their efficient use can ensure completion of a job with reasonable rewards for the contractor, and the operatives, in addition to providing the client with a satisfactory product. And the successful achievement of this situation is surely the primary object of those engaged in industrial relations.

The Happy-worker Theory

Unfortunately, this truism is not always clearly recognized in the construction industry. Not infrequently it is said that the

[8] *Organization of Building Sites*, p. 73, National Building Study Report No. 29, H.M.S.O.

pursuit of "happiness" is the major objective! Closer examination reveals that this is based on the presumption that "a happy worker is an efficient worker". This is one of those phrases which has about it the ring of profundity; in fact it often has little relation to reality. Building operatives do not go to work in the hope of achieving positive happiness but in order to earn money which they may use to pursue happiness in other directions of their own choice!

This comment about the "happiness theory" is not intended to deride those who believe this the object of good industrial relations, or the perpetrators of the many press advertisements promising that: "You Will be Happier Working at Blank's Factory!" The purpose is to emphasize that, apart from any controversy over the theory itself, industrial-relations techniques must be adapted to meet the requirements of different industries. In a stable manufacturing firm the employer may attempt to keep his workers "happy" by providing music-while-you-work, clean and well-furnished rest rooms and restaurants, facilities for drama and other cultural group activities and perhaps sports fields. Gold watches and other presentations may also mark the long service of his employees to the firm.

These are fringe benefits which may well help achieve better relations between employer and employees—though quite clearly they will not replace monetary earnings as the major deciding factor. In the construction industry this earnings factor is of even greater significance because the casual nature of employment suffered by building workers makes it difficult even for the most progressive employers to provide amenities comparable to those in factory work. In these circumstances the earnings factor is a crucial one for those whose job it is to promote good industrial relations in the construction industry, and a consideration to be firmly fixed in their minds. Of course, it has been frequently suggested by both union officials and management that the real answer is to decasualize the industry so that extension of fringe benefits become possible.

In the last few years attention has, in fact, been increasingly concentrated on this aspect. A pilot survey into "The Degree of Continuity of Operative Employment" has been sponsored by the Ministry of Public Building and Works in conjunction with the Ministry of Labour and the economic development committees for building and civil engineering. The survey was undertaken by a department of the London School of Economics and their objective was to discover the extent of the problem and the main factors affecting it.

The research team made its report towards the end of 1966. It emphasized that the survey covered only a small number of firms and it took place during the 5-week period from 23 March 1966. Obviously any data arising from such a restricted survey both in time and scope has limited value as the authors themselves point out. They add that, because of this, the report may therefore ask "as many questions as it answers, but it is hoped in this way to clarify the direction in which further research and discussion should be aimed".

A number of valuable suggestions are made for more detailed investigation and are being seriously examined by the various interests involved in the construction industry. Increasing factory production of industrialized building components; extension generally of "dry" types of construction; the national registration of building operatives—all these are proposals put forward in the hope that they would help to decasualize the industry.

But, even accepting that their implementation would assist to some extent, we are still left with the basic operational system of the industry. It has to produce an immensely varied range of products and the production system must be taken from site to site as the client dictates. Nor can builders guarantee continuity of employment to their operatives when, due to the vagaries of the tendering system and the economic climate, they themselves have no guarantee of continuity of employment for their own capital resources.

What must be recognized, therefore, is that, while there is a great deal which can be done to regularize the industry, it is likely to retain the unenviable reputation of having the highest degree of casualization, with the consequent risk this involves both for employees and employers. The worker faces insecurity and has annual earnings which are generally below the national average. The employer risks his capital in an industry which is extremely hazardous and where profit margins are lower than in many others.

Top of the Bankruptcy Tables

The annual reports on bankruptcy from the Board of Trade provide sad evidence of the consequences for men and employers. Each year a number of building employees are declared bankrupt (95 in 1965) and, as is well known from press reports, builders continually top the list of business failures. What is not so clearly understood is that press reports usually underestimate the position, for, in the Board of Trade tables, the term "builders" is used strictly to denote firms classifying themselves as such. It does not include the failures of other firms in the industry such as plumbing, plastering and painting contractors.

One therefore reads that the table showing "Failures in the principal trades" for 1965 puts "Builders" well at the top with 392, followed by "Directors and promoters of companies" with the much lower figure of 165. It is when we add to the total of bankruptcies among builders the failures of other firms in the industry that we see the true position. Bankruptcies of businesses operating in the construction industry form a very high—and increasing—percentage of the total number of bankruptcies, as shown by Table 6.[9]

Of course, it could be maintained that bankruptcy is the consequence of inefficiency rather than risk, and then all that the table proves is that construction industry firms are less efficient than others. No doubt many failures in the industry were due to inefficiency but there are also firms of good repute, and with

[9] This table is taken from the *Monthly Bulletin of Statistics*, July 1966, published by the Ministry of Public Building and Works.

TABLE 6. BANKRUPTCIES

Year	Firms in construction	Total no. of firms	Construction firms as percentage of the total
1960	374	3220	11·7
1961	463	3946	11·7
1962	562	4601	12·2
1963	615	4370	14·1
1964	567	3766	15·1
1965	574	3760	15·3

years of existence behind them, which have found themselves in trouble because of the vagaries of the industry and the conditions in which they have to operate. The figures for 1963, in which there was a severe freeze-up, clearly substantiate this point. Though the total number of bankruptcies in Britain during that year fell slightly compared with 1962, those in construction went up to 615 which is the highest figure for any of the 6 years shown in the table.

This problem, and the others dealt with in this chapter, have been expounded to show that there are great difficulties in the construction industry facing management and unions in their attempts to achieve greater efficiency and improve industrial relations. Those who take a critical view of the level of attainment in these fields should remember this fact. It is also essential to understand the background of such a complex industry to comprehend fully the way in which the union and employer organizations have developed and gradually evolved their particular systems of joint consultation.

CHAPTER 3

History of the Unions

A Vital Freedom

The existence of trade unions signifies a very vital freedom within this country—the rights of workpeople to free negotiation on their conditions of employment. This, in essence, is the difference between a free man and a slave. And though most people seem to assume that these rights are part of a long British democratic tradition, they have existed for only 143 years out of the last 2000 years which we look upon as reasonably modern history.

Because of this relatively limited period of "legality", written union histories rarely venture back much before the beginning of the nineteenth century. In fact it is often claimed—with some justification—that the pre-conditions necessary for the creation of stable trade unions date mainly from the period of the Industrial Revolution. For the new discoveries and inventions which developed manufacturing industry on a large scale signified the end of the medieval craft guild system. "It is not until the changing conditions of industry had reduced to an infinitesimal chance the journeyman's prospect of becoming himself a master that we find the passage of ephemeral combinations into permanent trade societies" wrote the Webbs in their *History of Trade Unionism*.

This was a reasonable assumption to make against the general concept that, until the Industrial Revolution, commodities were normally produced in small establishments controlled by a master employing a few craftsmen and apprentices who mainly used handcrafts rather than machinery. Within such a system of

29

production the apprentice could also look towards the possibility of proceeding through the journeyman stage to becoming a master in his own right. This situation meant that there was common identity of interest between these classes which greatly lessened the possibility of conflict.

The Industrial Revolution, with its large scale production, brought into being a new class of workers who fully realized they had little prospect of personal advancement. On the other hand, the working conditions of these employees, and their close proximity within the new industrial establishments, gave them an identity of interest as a single class and also the opportunity to form organizations to give voice to their grievances.

If we accept the logic of these arguments about the pre-conditions necessary for the existence of unions, there immediately arises a significant question about developments within the building industry. For the building of castles, palaces and buildings of religious worship must obviously have involved large numbers of building workers congregated together for a long time on a particular site. In addition to this the histories of the early building industry make it quite clear that the great majority of operatives were firmly placed in the employee category with little prospect of themselves becoming employers. It might well be that—under the direction of a client—a thousand masons, carpenters and other building workers would be employed on a single large project, such as the construction of Windsor Castle, for many years.

The building industry, therefore, had for centuries operated under the kind of conditions that other workers were only now beginning to experience due to the impact of the Industrial Revolution. The essential pre-conditions for common trade action among building workers were there—and historical records indicate that it certainly took place. One of the first major regulations governing wages was the Statute of Labourers in 1349. It was implemented as the consequence of the plague, or the Black Death as it commonly became known, which killed off a considerable part of the country's labour force. The law of supply and demand was, as a consequence, tipped greatly in favour of the worker and he was obviously in the position of being able to exercise greater influence on his conditions of employment. To prevent workers taking advantage of this situation, one which neither the Government nor the employers desired, the Statute of Labourers declared that the State was the supreme arbiter on wages and workers should not be paid a higher rate of wages than was customary in the year before the Black Death. This Statute therefore made it illegal for workers to attempt to combine together and negotiate their wage rates, and heavy penalties were laid down for those offending against the intentions of the Statute.

That there was strong opposition from building workers to this and other statutes is evident from the passing of further legislation in 1351, 1360 and 1425 in which building workers were specifically condemned because, as the statutes declared, they had attempted to push their wages above the lawful limits. Perhaps the most significant comment about these early combinations is that of J. Wycliffe who complained in the fourteenth century that masons "conspire together that no man of their craft shall take less for a day than they fix though he should by good conscience take much less; that none of them shall do good steady work which might interfere with the earnings of other men of the craft, and that none of them shall do anything but cut stone, though he might profit his master twenty pounds by one day's work by laying a wall, without harm to himself".[1]

Leaving aside Wycliffe's rather startling assumption of the profit to be made for one day's honest toil by a mason—£20 in the fourteenth century!—the complaint certainly indicates that the masons had set up organizations which were influencing both wages and output. Nor did the later statutes against them appear to make them any less vigorous, even though penalties became more severe. In 1563 one brought in under Elizabeth consolidated all previous statutes relating to labourers and ruled that local magistrates would be the only persons empowered

[1] L. F. Salzman, *Building in England*, p. 42.

to fix wage rates. Penalties were specified for workers who transgressed and a persistent offender was to be fined £40, put in the pillory and also have one of his ears removed!

It should be emphasized here that the law was not simply against combinations in themselves. Associations of craftsmen and others might well exist for certain purposes, but it would be illegal if they had as the ostensible objective the influencing of wages and conditions as these powers lay with the local magistrates. It was a later Act, that of 1799, which was to make the Act of Combination in itself illegal.

Towards the end of the eighteenth century it was no secret that wage regulation by magistrates had largely fallen into disuse over the years and workers were beginning to form effective unions to represent their grievances to the employers. This was a situation which pleased neither the employers nor the government. The complaint generally raised by the employers was that the new organizations being formed by workmen, or conspiracies as the employers frequently alleged, were attempting to enforce trade rules which "were in restraint of trade". This was a very serious offence at a time when British industry was expanding rapidly and attempting to capture the markets of the world. The retort of the workmen was that they were fighting to prevent themselves being completely degraded. Nor was the conflict confined to the newly emerging factory industries. In agriculture new methods had also been adopted which made it possible to reap high returns for capital invested provided the old system of cultivation, where tenants tilled their own strips of land and held certain grazing rights in common, was eliminated. This elimination of peasants' rights and the creation of larger areas of land under a single ownership was mainly brought about by the extensive use of Enclosure Acts. Under these Acts great numbers of the peasantry were dispossessed of their land and the result was serious hardship for them.

This internal struggle between the classes in the industrial and the agricultural areas was being fought at a time when Britain was waging a bitter war against France; a France which was now a republic as the result of a bloody revolution generally regarded by historians as one of the most outstanding events of the eighteenth century. At home the government feared that the spirit of the revolution had crossed the narrow strip of water separating France from England and greatly influenced working-class opinion in Britain. It was almost inevitable that the government was apprehensive in case the French experiment might be repeated on British soil. Combinations of working men might not simply be defensive organizations related to their working conditions, but the basis from which positive action might be taken towards achieving a total revolution on the French pattern.

Combinations Acts

It was this fear by the state on one hand and the agitation of the employers on the other which brought about the passing of the Combinations Act of 1799 (slightly amended in 1800 due to the antagonism it provoked), which had the ostensible objective of outlawing combinations of workers—and also employers. The Act of 1799 was, in fact, the consolidation of all the legislation going back to the first Statute of Labourers forbidding workers the right to form unions within trades, with the intention of influencing their wages and conditions.

Though the masters were supposedly also brought within the terms of the Combinations Acts, to give them the appearance of fairness, the realism of the situation which prevailed was quite different. In fact it remained the same system which the famous economist Adam Smith had criticized some years before in his *Wealth of Nations*. He wrote then: "We have no Acts of Parliament against combining to lower the price of work, but many against combining to raise it." He claimed that:

> When masters combine together in order to reduce the wages of their workmen, they commonly enter into a private bond or agreement, not to give more than a certain wage under a certain penalty. Were the workmen to enter into a contrary combination of the same kind, not to accept a certain wage under a certain penalty, the law would punish them very severely; and if it dealt impartially it would treat the masters in the same manner.

The fact that the Government continued to exercise partiality was never in doubt. Though many workmen were punished for offences under the Combinations Acts, there appears to be no case on record of enforcement brought against an employer. This situation, however, did not lead to the destruction of all the early trade unions or curb the desire of workmen to combine in defence of their rights. The major effect of the new legislation was that it probably delayed the growth of more widespread organization and, of course, it had the result of forcing "the movement underground to some extent, thus giving to these labourers' brotherhoods and clubs some of that very character of seditious confederacies which it had been feared that they might assume, and also, by making joint agreements between masters and their men illegal, giving to all such negotiations an atmosphere of insecurity".[2]

The Combinations Acts remained in force for 25 years until the Repeal Act of 1824 (amended slightly in 1825). This Repeal was due not only to constant pressure from the trade unions and radical opinion generally, but also because a more settled general atmosphere now existed in the country. The Industrial Revolution was an accomplished fact, and war with France and the concomitant fear of political revolution at home was now over.

With the repeal of the Combinations Acts it is said that many unions immediately sprang into existence. It would probably be more accurate to say that, for a large number of them, it simply meant that they could "emerge into the daylight" without running the risk of prosecution which had previously threatened them. Certainly the building unions which made themselves effective in the immediate post-repeal period did not act as if they were newly formed, naive and inexperienced organizations. Instead they bore that quality of militancy and independence against which all the statutes over the last 500 years had complained.

For example, the carpenters employed on the building of Buckingham Palace in 1825 showed their lack of awe for this

[2] A. F. Fremantle, *England in the Nineteenth Century*, George Allen & Unwin, p. 197.

project of national prestige by bringing the men out on strike. Their vigorous attempts to keep black-legs away from the site led to almost battle-like conditions ended, appropriately enough, by bringing the Coldstream Guards into action against them.[3]

The carpenters, of course, like the masons, bricklayers and other building craftsmen, were among the aristocracy of the artisan class and they demonstrated this by their early entry into the trade-union struggle. This does not mean that they immediately possessed well-organized and widespread unions on the pattern we know today. Travelling was not very easy in those days and communications generally were more difficult. These conditions, together with other contemporary circumstances, meant that early unions were generally restricted in scope. And even within the boundaries of a small town it cannot be presumed that union branches would encompass the whole area. In fact "organization" might be confined to the men in a particular shop or yard and grievances against the employers put forward by way of a "round robin" petition rather than by formal trade-union representation.

1560220

The First "National" Unions

It was only gradually that the operatives began to form unions of a more broadly based nature and it was not until 1827, with the foundation of the General Union of Carpenters, and Joiners, at a meeting in London, that we have any record of an attempt at wide-scale building trade unionism. The Carpenters' and Joiners' Union was followed in 1829 by the formation of the Friendly Society of Bricklayers at a meeting in Manchester. Although few records remain of its early years it probably had its main centres of strength—as had most other unions—in the Midlands and London. The third union of a national character which was created was the Operative Stonemasons' Society in 1831. This particular union expanded very rapidly and, within 2 years, had reached the then exceptional total of nearly 4000 members enrolled in 100 branches that stretched from Carlisle in the north right

[3] R. W. Postgate, *The Builders' History*, p. 52.

down to Plymouth in the south.[4] It was recognized as the most powerful British union of its day and, in any building industry battle, was regarded as one of the most "militant and aggressive regiments in Labour's army".

By 1831 other attempts at wider organization had also been made among the painters, plumbers and glaziers, plasterers, slaters and other trades. Though the resulting unions often had the prefix "national" attached to their names, they were perhaps even less extensive or powerful than those of the carpenters and joiners, the stonemasons and the bricklayers. And the aggregate membership of all of these building unions formed only a minor percentage of the industry's total labour force and membership was confined to craftsmen. Among labourers there appear to have been no attempts at organization during the immediate years after repeal of the Combinations laws. This also seems to be the situation which applied in other industries for, as the Webbs explained:

> The formation of independent associations to resist the will of the employers required the possession of a certain degree of personal independence and strength of character. Thus we find the earliest trade unions arising among journeymen whose skill and standard of life had been for centuries encouraged and protected by legal or customary regulations as to apprenticeship, and by the limitation of their members which the high premiums and other conditions must have involved.[5]

Independence and strength of character the early building trade unionists certainly possessed, even if these qualities were not backed by mass organization. That they also possessed remarkable vision is revealed by their attempt in 1832 to go beyond the limits of mere craft organization and establish a powerful federation of all the crafts which, they felt, the employers would be unable to resist. In that year they formed a federal organization called the Operative Builders' Union (OBU) which was based on affiliation from some of the most powerful unions in the industry. The main object of the OBU was: "To advance and equalise the price of labour in every Branch of the trade we admit into this society."

[4] W. S. Hilton, *Foes to Tyranny*, p. 26.
[5] *History of Trade Unionism*, p. 44.

Though the basis of a strong fighting organization now existed, the first conflict entered by the OBU amounted, however, almost to a farce. Making it even more bizarre was the fact that the enemy the OBU was forged to fight—the small master class— took part in it at the side of the unions. This peculiar situation arose because their common adversary was the general contractor, now beginning to spread throughout the industry. The craftsmen could see many dangers for them in this system. The general contractor would probably be a more remote and harder task-master, and less sympathetic to their claims than the small craft employer who had usually risen from the ranks of the journeymen. The enmity of the masters to the general contractor arose from the fears that their own status and hard-earned capital were in jeopardy. Unions and masters therefore united under the banner "that no new building should be erected by contract with one person".

The Document

Looked at objectively, an attempt was being made to hold back an inevitable development in the industry; it was certain to fail in the long run. Yet, in a few localities, the joint demands of the OBU and the masters were apparently met by some clients and this was sufficient for the OBU to believe that a major victory had been won. It was with increased confidence, therefore, that they now turned on the masters and demanded a number of industrial reforms including a uniform wage for "each class of operatives, a limitation of apprentices, the prohibition of machinery and piecework, and other requirements special to each branch of the trade". These claims were completely unacceptable to the masters and they now realized that their joint interests lay in crushing the OBU while this was still possible, otherwise it might develop into a powerful machine able to force its will upon them. Their answer to the OBU, therefore, was a counter-demand that their employees should sign a formal declaration (which later became notoriously known in the industry as "The Document") stating that: "We, the undersigned do hereby declare that we are not in any way connected with the General Union of the Building Trades and that we do not and will not contribute to the support of such members of the said Union as are or may be out of work in consequence of belonging to such Union."

The employers must have known that this was really a declaration of war on their part, and it was certainly accepted as such by the unions affiliated to the OBU. In Liverpool union members immediately refused to sign "The Document" and the strike began in that area. It soon spread to Birmingham, Manchester and then throughout the Midlands generally. It was a major battle in which both sides were now engaged; but what was the condition of the antagonists? The masters had no stable organization and had only recently come together and overcome their mutual distrust because of their greater common fear of the OBU. That organization, however, was still very much in its infancy and depended upon the support of affiliated unions which were, themselves, far from being stable organizations. Some of them had only come into existence a few months before the formation of the OBU. And those visionary ideals which had helped them create their federation were to become so powerful, and out of proportion to the means of carrying them into effect, that they soon found themselves with little control of the general situation. The man who helped urge them in the direction of organizational suicide was Robert Owen, a well-known radical mill owner with great sympathy for the sufferings of the working class. He thought that the solution to their problems lay in the formation of co-operative types of endeavour.

He regarded the establishment of the OBU as the most progressive step yet taken within the trade-union movement—which it was—and decided that it was the right vehicle for advancing his ideals of a co-operative commonwealth. To this end he met the delegates of unions affiliated to the OBU at a special conference and put his arguments to them with great force and persuasion. He pronounced a simple solution to all their conflicts with the employers. They could shake off their shackles merely by forming co-operative productive units to work directly for the public. There would be no employer class and, consequently, there would be no conflict.

To the unions the matter seemed so completely simple, and so final a solution to their problems, that Owen's vision and theirs combined enthusiastically. They agreed to divert a portion of their limited funds and energies to found a National Building Guild which was to have its Guild Hall in Broad Street, Birmingham. It seemed not to matter to them that this decision was taken at the same time as their struggle was intensifying with the employers and the OBU was now, in reality, fighting for its existence on the issue of The Document.

The truth was that no longer was it a question of whether the OBU could win the struggle and survive, but for how long it could stave off the inevitable catastrophe. In fact it was all over by 1834. The OBU was dead and the National Building Guild with it. Some of the unions involved in the disaster had been completely shattered. Others, like the carpenters, masons and bricklayers, retreated with the battered remnants of their unions into craft isolation and began the slow struggle back to organizational health. The disaster had such an effect on union thinking that it was to be another 84 years before they again committed themselves to the principle of federation.

But there were union officials then, as now, who lived by the maxim that any setback is only temporary and that no defeat is complete. At worst there are lessons to be learned which will help more stable development in the future. So it was with the end of the OBU. The remaining unions recognized the structural weaknesses which had been exposed and began to rectify them within their own craft organizations. One of the major defects had been the reluctance of branches to give money or power to a central administration, about which they were suspicious and over which they felt they had little control. This was gradually overcome—at least as far as monetary contributions were concerned—and consequently the first few full-time general secretaries were appointed, though in nearly every case they had neither staff nor offices and had to work from their homes. Over strikes the central administration still exercised little control, although it was recognized that uninhibited strike action was bound to drain away union finances and put the whole organization at risk. Nevertheless, the establishment of full-time secretaries was a major step in the right direction and from them to the branches went out newsletters giving information relating to strikes, work-possibilities and finances. These newsletters, providing a vital link between branches, were the forerunners of our present union journals.

During the years after the crash of the OBU this was the general pattern of development, though it certainly was far from being smooth and without inter-union conflict. For a while some of the new unions which were established resulted from efforts at drawing together various autonomous craft branches, other unions were the result of conflict leading to a fragmentation of organization. In 1847, for example, the Friendly Society of Bricklayers ran into financial troubles and the consequential acrimony led to the establishment of two separate "orders" of bricklayers which became known as the Manchester Order, and the London Order.

Among the new unions which gradually evolved there was established the Associated Society of Carpenters and Joiners in 1860, followed 6 years later by the foundation of the Mill Sawyers. The painters also made another attempt at widespread organi-zation in 1856 when the Manchester Alliance of Painters was established as the result of amalgamation of several small societies. The plasterers, who had also had their earlier union shattered in the destruction of the OBU, formed the National Association of Operative Plasterers in 1860; and the plumbers got over their setback and settled on a more stable basis with the creation of the United Operative Plumbers' Association in 1865.

Strike Control

Many local autonomous units still remained, of course, and even the major organizations continued to undergo changes in administration and names due to quarrels, amalgamations or financial difficulties. The thread of each of their histories is a tortuous one and these often reflected in their changing shapes and patterns the changes which were taking place in the industry itself. One sign of this was the continuing strikes against the introduction of machinery or any other innovation which the craftsmen thought might demean their skill and their status. In addition to this the unions were making efforts to shorten the length of the working day, especially in winter, because of the craftsmen's opposition to "the detested practice of working by candlelight".

Most of the strikes took place on a localized basis and often against a particular employer. Sometimes there was so many of them taking place at the same time that the central committees of the various unions decided that, if the safety of the organizations were to be ensured, branches must now obey some form of control in relation to strike action. The rules which were generally evolved required that branches should submit prior application to the central committee for permission to strike, and in many cases the committee would subsequently put the question to a vote of the union's entire membership. What they were asked in these national ballots was, in effect: "Are you prepared to allow a certain branch to strike for a stated aim and be supported by strike pay out of central funds?" In some cases, when the general financial position of the union was taken into consideration, the answer had to be in the negative.

The branches, which had only reluctantly accepted the necessity of financial support for central control, did not always take kindly to this further need for sacrificing their power of strike decision. Yet this was an essential step if the unions were to become more stable and powerful. This early resistance to the idea of central direction of strike action is perhaps best shown by the comment of the members of the Coventry Branch of the Operative Stonemasons' Society when, in 1837, their General Secretary tried to "cool off" their ardour for battle with the employers.

"Good God, is it inconsistent in working men to better their conditions?" the branch thundered in reply. "Men who are the real producers of wealth: men who, after toiling and bleeding to keep a set of lazy and indolent plunderers in luxury, are very frequently doomed to pass their declining years in some accursed bastille, or in obscurity, starvation and wretchedness! Ah! worthy brothers, we have hitherto been used worse than brutes, let us now strive to be men."

This outburst from Coventry is also revealing of the decline taking place in the status of building craftsmen and the general social conditions which then existed. The more farsighted union leaders were well aware of the situation, but they were torn between their desire to fight for better conditions and the necessity for building up the strength of their unions which they knew could easily be destroyed by uninhibited strike action. The Operative Stonemasons' Society, for example, nearly extinguished itself when it waged a 9 months' strike during the building of the Houses of Parliament (also bringing Nelson's Column and Woolwich Dockyard into the dispute) in 1841.

Other unions also struck against employers in conflicts which were extended over many months. Two of the major demands of the building workers at that time were for shorter working hours, and for the retention of the customary system of payment-by-the-day instead of the hourly payment which the employers were trying to force upon them. In the major industrial centres there was always some dispute taking place over these two vital principles.

The Working Rules

After some years of almost constant challenge on these issues the net result might well be described as a draw. The unions were successful in their attempts to shorten the length of the working day but the employers could claim that they had managed to impose payment by the hour.

By 1900, therefore, the main basis of the industry's working rules had been established. The unions had also undergone the changes necessary to stabilize their administration. Originally formed with the single aim of agitating for better conditions, they were now offering their members what amounted to a rather primitive system of social security by providing sickness, accident and disablement benefits.

Even among the labourers, largely neglected during the formation of the earlier unions, various attempts at organization had been made. It was with the setting up of the United Builders' Labourers' Union in 1889, however, that the first really stable organization was created catering specifically for labourers in the industry.[6] The organizing of labourers was not the only significant change in the trade union scene at the turn of the century. For the Operative Stonemasons, long the premier union in the industry, had reached its zenith and had begun the gradual decline which reflected the diminishing use of stone within the industry in favour of other materials.

The early years of union struggle, and the mistakes which were made, had also led to an increasing awareness among the members of some of the major unions that individual trade organization was not enough. Amalgamation of all the trades, or at least a new attempt at federation, should be made to create a strong organization which would be capable of resisting the attempts to cut wages and conditions as the general economic situation began to decline in Britain. The amalgamationists—as they became known —had set themselves a task which was far from easy. Though stronger national organizations now existed, and the borders of Scotland and Ireland had been successfully crossed in some cases, anything up to 100 autonomous unions still operated within the industry.

However, the London Order of Bricklayers decided to force the pace and announced the setting up of a provisional committee "for the consolidation of the trade unions within the building industry". As a preliminary basis for its campaign it succeeded in having a motion carried at the 1911 Trades Union Congress

[6] This organization was later to become known as the National Builders' Labourers' and Construction Workers' Society. It amalgamated with the AUBTW in 1952.

approving the objective of "amalgamating the several Trade Unions with each industry".

Amalgamation, however, did not meet with universal favour. Paying lip-service to the idea but in practice against it were some full-time officials who obviously feared for their status and jobs if the one-union goal were achieved. There was also some opposition from members because, in their own craft unions, they had built up favourable friendly benefits which they thought might depreciate if a common denominator were applied through amalgamation. Nevertheless, the amalgamationists managed to persuade several unions to the point of balloting their members on the issue. Though the first vote on the general principal was carried it was obvious, when it came to the later and more vital ballot on details such as the administration and scale of friendly benefits, that the amalgamation attempt was doomed to failure. But, like other apparent union failures, this was one of those which sparked off attempts at the available alternatives.

The first and obvious one was for a closely knit federation between the trades. This would allow for a high degree of uniformity of action while preserving autonomous rights for each organization. Secondly, those unions which felt adventurous enough could still aim at amalgamation between themselves. The final alternative, and one on which some members became very firmly resolved, was to set up a new industrial union which would cater for all building operatives. The few years after the abortive attempt at general amalgamation were, therefore, ones of considerable activity and development within the building unions as these various objectives were propagated.

The first move was the setting up, by those members who had enthusiastically adopted the concept of a new industrial union, of an organization called the Building Workers' Industrial Union in 1914. They claimed this to be the complete answer to the original amalgamation failure. Simply create an industrial union, enrol any trade in it, and finally the goal would be reached in any case. However, conditions at the time were against any possible chance of it succeeding in attaining its objectives. In the same year the

Great War began and this made union organization difficult—
especially for so new an enterprise. Even more fatal to its chances
of survival was the fact that the leaders of all the established
unions expressed outright hostility. This was all that was required
to finally kill the attempt at industrial unionism. Nevertheless, it
drove some leaders to the realization that some form of unity was
required and they finally took the necessary steps to bring into
being the National Federation of Building Trades Operatives
in 1918.[7]

Other significant developments which arose out of the fluidity
of ideas within this particular period were the creation of the two
largest building unions now in existence by the process of amalgamation in 1921. In that year the General Union of Carpenters
and Joiners linked up with the Amalgamated Society of Carpenters and Joiners to form the Amalgamated Society of Woodworkers (ASW); and the London Order of Bricklayers, together
with the Manchester Order, and the Operative Stonemasons, came
together in the Amalgamated Union of Building Trade Operatives
(AUBTW).

The Strike of 1924

Only 3 years later these two new unions were, with the others
in the industry, to take part in what was up till then the only
national strike that had occurred in construction. This particular
dispute had its origins in a union claim for $2d.$ per hour increase on
wage rates. This the employers bluntly rejected pointing out that
the operatives had just received $\frac{1}{2}d.$ per hour increase under the
Sliding Scale Agreement. After some months of wrangling the
employers finally agreed to bring this up to $1d.$ per hour and it
looked as if industrial war had been narrowly avoided. Then the
employers decided to add other conditions as part of the settlement. They insisted that the union executives should forcibly
terminate a strike involving the Liverpool area and, in general,

[7] The history of this period is dealt with more fully in the next chapter
on the National Federation of Building Trades Operatives.

make sure that their members toed the line where the National Working Rules were concerned. While the unions were reluctantly prepared to settle for having the cost-of-living increase made up to a 1*d.* they angrily rejected these additional terms. In reply the employers threatened a lock-out on 5 July 1924, to "enforce discipline and the observance of agreed working rules".[8]

The answer of the unions to this threat was inevitable. They called on their members to begin a national strike on the same day as the declared lock-out—and to continue the strike until the employers had agreed to the terms laid down by the unions. Only after 7 weeks of conflict, followed by a court of enquiry appointed by the Minister of Labour, was the issue settled. Wage rates were increased by $\frac{1}{2}d.$ per hour making up the originally agreed total of a penny; summer working hours were to be $46\frac{1}{2}$ per week, while 44 applied in the winter; and London and Liverpool were to be given further consideration as "special areas" (the status which they have today).

The building unions congratulated themselves on having got through their first national strike reasonably successfully and prepared their organizations for the nationwide struggle which was threatening to arise from the situation in the coalmining industry. This threat became reality with the declaration of the 1926 General Strike. It was decided that the "front line" of workers pulled out should consist of the transport and heavy industries, including construction. For all its prominence in historical record this strike lasted only 9 days, was largely abortive, and its early ending led to considerable acrimony between the building unions. George Hicks, then the General Secretary of the AUBTW, and also a member of the TUC General Council, especially came under fire because he was "one of the guilty men who had betrayed the workers by calling off the strike".

But the General Strike, and the speed with which it was terminated, was partially attributable to the same cause—the rapidly deteriorating position of the British economy and the consequent depression of living standards for the workers. This situation was

[8] W. S. Hilton, *Foes to Tyranny*, p. 234.

summarized by Professor G. D. H. Cole, who wrote: "The singularly misguided and disastrous return to the gold standard in 1925 on the basis of the pre-war gold and dollar value of the pound had seriously damaged British export trade, and had led to a demand that all wages be reduced in order to bring down British costs of production to a competitive level."[9]

As this depression deepened from 1926 into the "hungry thirties" the building unions found themselves fighting hard to prevent a drastic weakening of their own organizations and of the Federation. The amalgamationist and expansionist outlook had to be temporarily shelved. Because investment in housing and other forms of construction had fallen, unemployment in construction rose so drastically that it reached a figure of around 40 per cent in some trades. And as the unemployment total rose so the unions found their membership falling. It was not until around 1936, in fact, that the economic situation began to improve and gradually gather strength as the country prepared to mobilize for the Second World War in 1939. When it came the unions generally found themselves in a completely new environment. The Government needed their help and full co-operation in the waging of total war on fascism and, in return, it was prepared to give them status they had never enjoyed before.

The building unions especially achieved a new eminence for:

> during the Second World War, especially after Dunkirk, Great Britain almost ceased to be a country. It became instead akin to an aircraft carrier launching offensives against the enemy: a huge pillbox standing protectively against the nightly air-raids—ready to resist invasion from across the English Channel. And the transformation was achieved with bricks, mortar, concrete and steel. Aerodromes were laid down and coastal defences and air-raid shelters built by men in the building industry. After the nightly destruction by Hitler's bombers they were feverishly working round the clock, patching, repairing, ready for further onslaught.[10]

If sacrifices were asked for from the men in the construction industry they received, in return, advances in wages and working conditions some of which they had been striving after for years.

[9] G. D. H. Cole, *A Short History of the British Working Class Movement*, p. 425.
[10] W. S. Hilton, *Foes to Tyranny*, p. 258.

And even though many building operatives were recruited to the armed forces the full employment situation resulted in the unions again gaining ground; financially they were much better off than they had been during the inter-war years. Some of them also took the opportunity during this period to strengthen their administration, and amalgamations even took place—such as that between the Building and Monumental Workers of Scotland with the AUBTW in 1942. Therefore, when peace was finally declared in 1945 the building unions were much stronger organizations than those which had faced up to the start of the conflict against Germany. Many of them had established the patterns of organization and structure which exist today. In some cases elected full-time executives administered the unions' affairs. On the whole it could be said that union administration had been expanded and improved. (Figure 1 shows the typical structure and administration of a large union within the building industry today.)

In the aftermath of the war the unions also found themselves with a bonus addition to their ranks. Not only did returning ex-servicemen rejoin, but many of the new entrants to the industry who had gone through government training courses—an overall target of 200,000 trainees had been set by the Labour Government—also became members. In addition to this, wages and conditions continued to improve and it seemed as if a golden era had begun. Certainly all the circumstances appeared ripe for an expansion of trade union strength and influence. Both major political parties had promised continuous and intensive investment in housing, educational, hospital and other forms of building. A large increase in the labour force was inevitable and the unions anticipated that an automatic consequence would be increased recruitment. Yet, within a relatively short time, they were to find a very disturbing downward trend in membership.

The "Birds of Passage"

There were union leaders, like Luke Fawcett, then the General Secretary of the AUBTW, who put the blame on an exodus of government trainees from the industry. "A realization that the builders life was not easy, the passing on of the birds of passage", he said, "all affected the position and the sudden influx was offset very largely by a sudden exodus."

Though this seemed a reasonable enough explanation at that time, it soon became clear that it accounted for only part of the problem. The grim fact which faced union leaders was that membership continued to decline in many of their organizations, and those that fared a little better made only marginal gains. This is

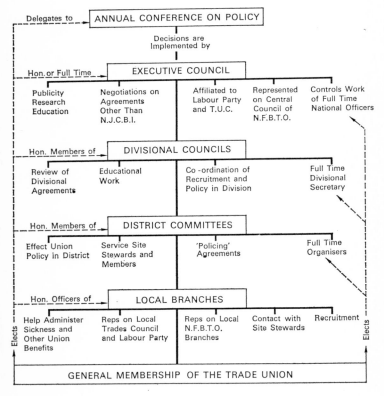

FIG. 2. A typical trade-union structure.

the situation which still exists today. Various explanations for it have been offered. One which is certainly true is that building unions have a much harder organizational task than those connected with other major industries. The constantly changing location of sites and the casual nature of employment—plus the large turnover in manpower with many thousands of men entering and leaving the industry each year—means that there is a greater ratio of organizing expenditure and energy necessary per operative than in other industries.

There is also the undeniable fact that the construction industry is becoming increasingly fragmented and an astonishingly rapid growth of self-employed personnel and labour-only sub-contracting is taking place. Harry Weaver, the present General Secretary of the NFBTO, has estimated that there may be a quarter million of these men now in the industry and makes the comment that they are obviously not the kind who are willing to take out trade-union membership.

One of the consequences of declining membership is that development of union administration and organization has been relatively slow in the last few years. It takes money to pay for such improvements and it is a bold union which, finding it difficult to prevent loss of members, radically raises subscriptions and consequently runs the risk of losing even more. The financial stringency resulting from this situation is such that only two of the major unions within the construction industry proper, the ASW and the AUBTW, employ research officers and carry out some kind of continuous educational work for their members. Some of the other unions find their membership and financial difficulties so considerable that advance is impossible and, in fact, retrenchment has taken place. Even pride of autonomy has, in some unions, taken a fall because of membership and financial troubles and this has led to mergers in some cases, though not all the recent negotiations on amalgamations are due to this fact.

Hopeful signs on the trade-union scene in the last few years are that the Amalgamated Society of Painters and Decorators has merged with the Scottish Painters' Society (and one or two other small autonomous painting unions) to form the first all British union catering for painters while the Packing Case Makers have gone into the ASW, and the National Association of Operative Plasterers has amalgamated with the Scottish Plasterers' Union.

The NFBTO has tried to encourage these developments with the ultimate objective of obtaining three major building union groupings, one for the wet trades, one for the dry-fixing trades, and one for plumbing and metal work. The first attempt to carry out these proposals was made among the wet-fixing trades and included seven unions catering for bricklayers, plasterers, masons, slaters and tilers, and asphalt workers. A number of meetings were held to establish first principles, but this admirable attempt at a logical amalgamation of closely related trades unfortunately failed.

The problems facing the unions, and their possible consequences, are serious not only for themselves but for the industry as a whole. Although some people still retain the misconception that unions exist solely for the purpose of agitating for increases in wages and conditions, this is no more true than that employers organizations exist solely for the purpose of creating resistance to this pressure. Negotiations over wages and conditions and occasional strikes take up only a small amount of trade-union time. In addition to the very large volume of other internal work, including the administration of the various benefits, the unions are in partnership with the employers on a wide range of important matters such as safety, health and welfare, apprenticeship and training in general.

At top level the union leaders participate in many government consultative committees, and others such as the economic development committees for building and civil engineering. At regional and local level, union officials and lay members are to be found on the boards of technical colleges, helping with apprenticeship training and serving on tribunals connected with various government ministries. The position is, therefore, that a considerable part of trade-union finances and energies go to serve the community in general rather than trade-union objectives in a narrow sense.

It has, in fact, been said that if trade unions did not exist it would be necessary to create them so they could carry out the wide variety of functions they now perform. Certainly the building unions can claim that with all the problems they face in their complex and constantly changing industry they have attempted to carry out their objectives in a reasonable manner. For instance, a major accusation against trade unions in general is that they are conservative in attitude, resistant to change and prone to indulge in restrictive practices. Here again the building unions can plead "not guilty", even though they represent men using some of the oldest handcrafts still exercised widely in British industry.

Perhaps the last word on this point can be left with the National Federation of Building Trade Employers, which has paid tribute to the work of the unions in general and especially that: "The industry is undergoing widespread technical change, but the building trade unions have not opposed the introduction of new methods, materials or machines as such. With the co-operation of the unions the National Joint Council for the Building Industry has been able, where necessary, to lay down principles to be followed in the adoption of new methods."[11]

[11] NFBTE: *Statement of Evidence to the Royal Commission on Trade Unions and Employers' Associations*, Par. 52.

CHAPTER 4

The National Federation of Building Trades Operatives

The Most Effective Federation

Accepted as the most compact and effective industrial federation of unions in Britain the National Federation of Building Trades Operatives partially owes its existence, ironically enough, to negative rather than positive action by certain building union leaders at the start of the twentieth century. Among them were the men who had fiercely opposed the attempt to establish the 1914 Building Workers' Industrial Union, which had lived for only a short time because of overwhelming antagonism against it.

It would be an over-simplification of the case, however, to portray all of the established trade union leaders as grim reactionaries solely determined to safeguard the existence of their own craft unions and, by inference, their own vested interests. In 1914 the building unions had just fought a hard and exhausting battle with the London employers when, once more, presentation of "The Document" had been one of the main points of contention. It was thought that for some members to break away at that particular moment, and to found a competing industrial union was tantamount to stabbing the others in the back.

Even John Batchelor, General Secretary of the London Order of Bricklayers (the organization which had led the struggle for all-out amalgamation), bitterly attacked the industrial unionists and commented that even though the London strike had been won, "it is regrettable to find at the moment of victory that a few of our members and of other Societies were so lost to their duty as to endeavour to start a rival society to, as they no doubt fondly hoped, complete the disintegration the builders had started".

With the London Bricklayers taking such a hostile attitude to the new organization it was obvious that the other unions, some of which had never favoured amalgamation in any case, would be even more antagonistic. An almost solid front of opposition was therefore presented to the Building Workers Industrial Union—even if the points of objection may have been rather varied. As a consequence a meeting of the established unions took place at which they discussed the general danger which could be posed by the new organization, and to consider the possibilities of closer liaison between themselves. The final result was a conference in London in February 1915 when they agreed to set up the National Association Building Trades Council (NABTC).

Even though this decision was based on a negative attitude, and perhaps reluctantly taken, the formation of the NABTC was a step in the right direction. The major resolution carried at its first meeting, however, revealed that the participating unions had rather narrow objectives in mind. "We recommend to the Executive Committees of this affiliated Society", it ran, "the necessity of refusing to recognise the cards of membership of newly formed unions which are in conflict with this Council and, if necessary, to be prepared to support each others members sustaining in this action."

The mere passing of this resolution, however, did not kill the desire among many union members for closer unity and action between the trades than was provided by the NABTC. In the course of time the leaders of the Council were therefore driven to examining ways in which this desire could be met, short of all-out amalgamation. They also found themselves subject to other pressures. Their Association was being given positive tasks to undertake, such as formulating policies to meet conditions in the industry when the Great War ended. Even to them, therefore, it soon became obvious that there was an urgent need for a much closer link to be forged than they had originally envisaged on the NABTC. The first society to make the necessary move to bring the matter to a head was the Amalgamated Society of Carpenters and Joiners which convened a meeting at which it put forward proposals for a much more tightly knit Federation. The union suggested that the title of the new organization might be the National Building Trades Federation.

Throughout 1916 and 1917 the details were thoroughly thrashed out by the unions affiliated to the NABTC then, on 5 February 1918, that Council met for the last time. After the formal business had been concluded it was unanimously resolved that: "This building trades council be, and the same is hereby, dissolved from this date, and those societies who have voted in favour of the federation scheme are hereby formed as the National Federation of Building Trades Operatives."[1]

It was one of the finest collective decisions that the building unions had taken in their long history. The new NFBTO was given such powers as would bring about uniformity of action among its affiliated organizations on wages, working conditions and other matters of common concern. And the powers that it was given this time were a reality—unlike those of the insecure and short-lived OBU in 1832—because they were supported by unions fully capable of sustaining the objectives of their new Federation.

These objectives, almost unchanged since the foundation of the NFBTO, are:

> To uphold the rights of combination of labour; to consolidate the affiliated Unions for common protection; to establish uniform rates of wages for all building trades operatives in the Construction Industry; to adjust disputes; to improve the general position of building trades operatives by securing unity of action amongst affiliated Unions; and to propagate the principle of control of industry by and for the benefit of the workers.[2]

The wide range of the Federation's declared objectives reveals just how far the isolationist nature of the affiliated unions had diminished; they were now prepared to give the Federation powers through joint decision which, only a few years previously, they

[1] W. S. Hilton, *Foes to Tyranny*, p. 217.
[2] *NFBTO General Rules*, p.5.

had been jealously hugging to themselves. Also, to many of the ardent amalgamationists the NFBTO was the next best alternative to their vision of an industrial union. Yet one of the peculiar by-products of the creation of the Federation was that it led to the founding of an industrial union within the industry existing alongside the already established organizations—a situation which they had been adamantly resisting only a few years before.

The Composite Section

This time, of course, there was a significant difference in that the organization of this union was confined to the rural areas, and its general control was in the hands of the affiliated trade unions through the NFBTO. This new industrial union was named the Composite Section of the NFBTO and its creation provided the solution to a recruiting problem which had faced the individual trade organizations ever since they began. As union structure is primarily based on the existence of local branches there have to be sufficient members of a trade within a given locality to justify the establishment of a branch. But in the rural areas a small town or village might only have one or two carpenters, bricklayers, painters, plumbers or other trades residing in them. The individual trade organizations therefore found themselves up against the obstacle that lack of members made traditional branch organization impossible.

The setting up of the Composite Section overcame this problem because every class of operative could be organized in its branches so that a workable unit was formed. Today the Composite Section has a membership of around 9000. During its 50 years of existence its total turnover, however, has probably been around 60,000 members. Without the creation of the NFBTO it could not have existed and many of the rural areas would have remained relatively unorganized. The individual trade unions have, therefore, had in the Composite Section a bonus arising out of their decisions to join together in the Federation. Within the Composite Section are two classes—"A" and "B"—of members. This rather unusual

division is due to the fact that the Section is regarded by the
Federation's affiliated unions as a recruiting instrument for the
strengthening of their own organizations. The "A" members are
those thought of as not being particularly connected with any one
affiliated union and are therefore subject to the Rules of the
Composite Section, "and under the direction and control of the
Central Council of the Federation" (Rule 12 (f)).

The "B" members are subject to "the control and authority of
the Executive Councils of the affiliated Unions to which they
respectively belong". In relation to these members the Composite
Section collects the contributions, deducts 15 per cent for administrative expenses, and forwards the balance to the appropriate
trade union. It is because of this unique set-up of the Composite
Section that it is not regarded as a trade union in its own right and
is therefore not affiliated to the Trades Union Congress.

Of course the basic objectives of the NFBTO have always been
to achieve unity of action among the unions on wages and working
conditions, and the Federation is the organization through which
the major relationships with the employers are now conducted.
Affiliated to the NFBTO are the twenty unions listed in Table 7,
including the Composite Section which for general purposes is
treated as an autonomous organization. One of the significant
points to note from Table 7 is that few of the unions affiliated to
the Federation do so on their total membership. Most affiliate on
the major part of their membership, and a smaller number on a
minor proportion of their membership. This is due to the fact that
even an organization like the Amalgamated Society of Woodworkers, which is often regarded as a purely building union, has a
large proportion of its members working in shipyards or in
factories unconnected with the construction industry. This is
also true of many of the other crafts.

Nevertheless, these are the ones which are basically linked to
the construction industry and they affiliate the largest part of their
membership to the NFBTO. On the other hand, the two general
workers' unions, and others like the National Union of Furniture
Trades Operatives, affiliate to the Federation only on that

relatively minor proportion of their membership which is actually working within the construction industry. To illustrate this point Table 7 shows the total membership of the unions attached to the Federation and the actual numbers on which they affiliate.

TABLE 7. NUMBER OF UNIONS AFFILIATED TO THE NFBTO; THE MEMBERSHIP ON WHICH THEY AFFILIATE TO THE NFBTO CONTRASTED WITH THAT ON WHICH THEY AFFILIATE TO THE TRADES UNION CONGRESS

Union	Membership Affiliated to the NFBTO	Membership Affiliated to the TUC
Amalgamated Slaters', Tilers' & Roofing Operatives' Society	2,012	2,012
Amalgamated Society of Painters & Decorators	60,011	74,064
Amalgamated Society of Woodcutting Machinists	8,000	26,365
Amalgamated Society of Woodworkers	121,856	191,620
Amalgamated Union of Asphalt Workers	2,000	3,000
Amalgamated Union of Building Trade Workers	80,100	76,260
Association of Building Technicians	900	2,000
Constructional Engineering Union	4,000	24,250
Electrical Trades Union	5,000	292,741
National Association of Operative Plasterers	10,781	10,781
National Society of Street Masons, P. & R.	1,200	1,400
National Union of Enginemen, Firemen, M. & E. Workers	1,500	30,000
National Union of Furniture Trade Operators	6,000	63,607
National Union of General and Municipal Workers	15,000	795,767
Plumbing Trades Union	30,000	55,615
Scottish Plasterers' Union	3,000	—
Scottish Slaters', Tilers', R. & C. Workers' Society	2,050	—
Transport & General Workers' Union	56,000	1,443,738
United French Polishers' Society	1,000	1,346
Composite Section (NFBTO)	7,500	—
Totals	417,910	3,094,566

Notes:

(a) The figures of affiliation to the NFBTO and the TUC are for December 1965.

(b) Table 7 shows twenty unions affiliated to the NFBTO at the end of 1965. Due to amalgamation between the AUBTW and the National Society of Street Masons and between the Scottish Plasterers Union and the National Association of Operative Plasterers the number of affiliated unions will decrease.

(c) No figures are shown for the two Scottish unions as these are affiliated to the Scottish TUC. The table also shows the AUBTW as having less members affiliated to the TUC than to the NFBTO. This is because the AUBTW, like all the other national unions, will have a separate number of members affiliated to the Scottish TUC while the NFBTO affiliations are for the entire national membership of its affiliated unions.

(d) No figure is shown of affiliations to the TUC by the Composite Section. As explained in this chapter the Composite Section is not regarded as a separate union and is therefore not affiliated to the TUC.

Affiliation fees to the Federation were, up to the 1 July 1964, based on a flat rate per member. However, it was protested that this was not really fair to the larger unions for, while they paid proportionally increasing fees, it could not be said that services to them necessarily increased in proportion. After a revision of the Rules in July 1964 a sliding scale of affiliation fees was applied and it is now laid down under Rule 5 of the Federation that:

> Affiliation fees to the Federation shall be in accordance with the following scale:
>
> 4/9 per member for the first 10,000,
> 4/4 per member for the second 10,000,
> 4/- for each additional member.

A significant fact which arises from this scale showing affiliation fees is that in comparison to that of other union federations they are quite heavy. The significance is that they reveal just how extensive the national, regional and local machinery of the Federation is and that a large income is required to sustain it.

The Central Council

The unions which are affiliated to the Federation make joint decisions determining the course of its policies through the governing authority of the Federation. For well over 40 years this body was known as the General Council. To this Council affiliated unions sent a limited number of delegates who took part in the discussions and made decisions affecting general Federation policies and administration. A situation then arose in which the Federation found itself having to call certain special meetings not covered by the constitution but certainly justified by circumstances. These meetings became known as the conferences of "joint executives".

The need to call such meetings arose because, on really vital matters affecting wages and conditions, the ordinary delegates at meetings of the General Council of the NFBTO felt that they did not possess immediate authority to take decisions. Usually they requested that they should be allowed to report back to their full union executives and then come back to the General Council having been briefed on how their executives wished them to vote. Obviously this was a cumbersome and time-consuming procedure so it was decided that, when important offers on wages and conditions were to be discussed, special meetings should be called to which the full executives of all the affiliated unions were invited. Debate could then take place followed by a brief suspension of the meeting while the various executives conferred about the way in which they should vote. Upon resumption of the meeting it was then possible to determine the issue by a show of hands or by a card vote.

It was finally realized that there was something superfluous in having a General Council which had such limited powers that it required, frequently, to be supported by the calling of these special joint executives meetings. As from July 1964, therefore, the previous rules were rescinded and it was decided that the new governing authority of the Federation should be called the Central Council and that: "The Central Council shall consist of the Executive Councils of affiliated societies. For the purpose of representation on the Councils, General Secretaries, Assistant General Secretaries and other full-time administrative officers, under the direct control of affiliated Executive Councils, shall be eligible." This change in the rule was an important one because it means that the full executives of affiliated unions can now attend the Central Council meetings and decisions on policy are made more speedily.

The Annual Conference

Central Council meetings are held in normal circumstances four times a year: "during the third week in March, June, September and December. The June meeting shall constitute the Annual meeting (known as the 'Annual Conference'), at which the term shall expire of the President, Vice-President and Executive Committee members, who shall be eligible for re-election."

From the above Rule 6 of the NFBTO it can be seen that the June meeting is regarded as the Federation's Annual Conference. While the other quarterly meetings might perhaps only take half a day to deal with their business, the June Conference usually takes place for almost a week. It has a full agenda of motions submitted from affiliated organizations to discuss, in addition to the election of its President, Vice-President and Executive Committee. This Conference is, in effect, the meeting at which the affiliated unions thrash out policy and administrative matters immediately affecting the Federation and also its future.

It is obvious, however, that an organization performing the wide range of work in which the NFBTO is involved—wage negotiations in private industry, local authorities and ministries, plus representation on various government and industrial committees—requires more detailed control than can be given by quarterly meetings of the Central Council. And though the role of the Central Council does include the occasional making of special decisions its major function is to lay down broad policy lines to be interpreted and implemented by the Executive Committee of the Federation. This E.C. meets at least once a month and is a very important part of the structure of the NFBTO.

Many vital decisions have to be taken on behalf of the Federation between the quarterly meetings of the Central Council and it is the E.C. which accepts this responsibility. The Executive consists of seven members who are elected at the June Annual

Conference of the Federation from nominees who must be accredited delegates to the Central Council. In addition to these seven members the President, Vice-President and General Secretary of the NFBTO also sit on the E.C. Because it plays such an important role within the Federation, and makes decisions affecting all of the unions, it is sought to ensure that its membership is broadly representative and Rule 3 (c) of the NFBTO states that: "No two members of one union shall be eligible to serve on the Committee, but no cognisance shall be taken of the Unions of which the President and the Vice-President are members."

The reference to the President and Vice-President is to allow for a situation where the elected President may, for example, come from the Amalgamated Society of Woodworkers but this does not bar another ASW delegate being nominated for one of the seven elective positions on the Executive Committee.

To keep affiliated unions closely in touch with the work and decisions of the E.C. the Federation's rules provide that: "Copies of the Executive Committee minutes shall be sent to the Head Offices of affiliated Unions and to the members of the Central Council of the Federation, and shall be presented to the next meeting of the Central Council for adoption." In fact, the major business of most of the Central Council quarterly meetings is to go through these sets of minutes item by item while delegates are given the chance to question any action that the E.C. may have taken in their name.

Another major function of the E.C. is generally to direct the work of the Federation's General Secretary, its chief full-time official. The General Secretary is elected by the Central Council and, whenever a vacancy arises for this position, each affiliated union is entitled to nominate a member of its own organization or of any other union affiliated to the Federation. Rather surprisingly, nominees for the general secretaryship need not have had any actual experience in membership of the Central Council. He can, in fact, be a lay-member straight from the site with the only qualification being that he must have had at least 10 years consecutive membership of his union. In actual practice, of course, this does not happen. The first secretary, Bill Bradshaw, was a union official when appointed. The man who followed him and held the position for over 40 years was Dick (now Sir Richard) Coppock. He had been a full-time official of the bricklayers when appointed to head the Federation's staff. When he retired in 1961 his total full-time union service was a world record unlikely ever to be broken. The man who succeeded Coppock, and presently is General Secretary, is Harry Weaver, who was full-time National President of the AUBTW at the time of his election.

After being elected the General Secretary remains in office without need to seek re-election so long as he performs his duties satisfactorily. As Rule 9 tastefully puts it, he "shall hold office at the pleasure" of the Central Council.

Under the direct control of the General Secretary is the head-office staff plus the full-time secretaries in each of the eleven regional areas of the NFBTO, together with their clerical assistants. It is this detailed organizational network, with a total full-time staff of around forty, which makes it the most comprehensive British union federation. Without its co-ordination of the strength of its affiliated unions, backing a commonly agreed line of action, it is very doubtful if building workers could have secured all the advances which they have achieved in their working conditions.

Administration of the NFBTO

The administrative structure of the Federation is a comprehensive one which reaches right down to local level where branches of the NFBTO may be formed in any particular locality "where two or more of the nationally affiliated Unions have branches in the district concerned." (A structural outline of the Federation is shown in Fig. 3.)

In outline the structure is relatively simple. Ultimate policy-making decisions rest with the affiliated unions who exercise this responsibility through their representatives on the Central Council, and particularly the Central Council meeting which is known

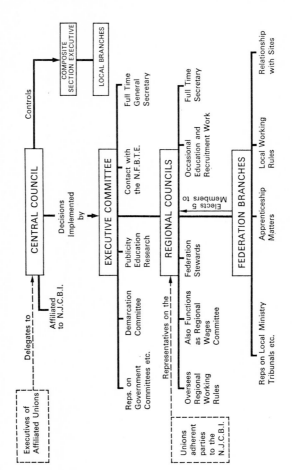

Fig. 3. Structure of the National Federation of Building Trades Operatives.

as the Annual Conference. Between meetings of the Council the control of the Federation lies with the Executive Committee which also gives general direction to the work of the General Secretary. In each of the eleven regions a Council of the Federation is in being to which is attached the local branches. The pattern of organization is one which provides for consultation and unity of action at all levels between the affiliated unions. A very important point also is that it provides for joint consultation at each level between the unions and the employers.

Apart from this consultative work at top level a great deal of important activity takes place on the regional councils. Regional councils of the NFBTO have been formed within areas defined as: "London; Southern Counties; South Western Counties; Eastern Counties; Midland Counties; South Wales and Monmouthshire; Yorkshire; North Western Counties; Northern (or North Eastern) Counties; Scotland; Ireland."

The duties of a regional council are generally to implement policy decided nationally by the Federation's Central Council and specifically to "deal with all building trade movements and disputes, infringements of the Working Rule Agreement and all questions affecting the Region arising from the National Joint Council Agreement".

Each regional council is comprised of members nominated by certain of the nationally affiliated unions and also five elected members from local Federation branches within the region. It is in the composition of the regional council representatives that an important distinction is revealed within the twenty unions which are affiliated to the NFBTO: those which are represented on the National Joint Council for the Building Industry (the organization which regulates wages and conditions in the private building sector) and those which are not. Out of the twenty unions eleven have representation on the National Joint Council and only these unions, in effect, have the right to vote within the Federation on matters which particularly relate to wages and conditions.[3]

[3] These unions are referred to in the section dealing with the structure of the National Joint Council.

These unions are therefore the only ones, under NFBTO Rules, which have the right to representation on the regional councils of the Federation. This is because one of the most important jobs of the regions is to liaise with the regional employers' organizations in deciding what regional variations should apply in the National Working Rules for the industry. In fact, Rule 11 (b) of the NFBTO makes this quite clear by establishing that: "The Regional Council of the Federation and the Regional Joint Wages Committee (Operatives' Side) under the National Agreement shall be merged into one body to be known as the Regional Council, which is to govern the district over which it has jurisdiction."

It is this aspect of the regional council's work which underlines the rule specifying that only those unions which are represented on the National Joint Council for the Building Industry have the automatic right to appoint delegates to the regional councils. This exclusiveness, however, is offset to some extent because the rule allows that, in addition to the direct union nominees, "there shall additionally be five members nominated and elected to the Regional Council by the Federation Branches within the regional area".

Through these additional five members those unions which are not represented on the National Joint Council for the industry are given the chance to participate in the work of the regional councils if their nominees at branch level are elected. All the regional councils of the Federation are constituted in this way except London and Northern Ireland which have slight variations to meet the particular circumstances in each of these regions.

Responsible for the conduct of the council's affairs is the Regional Secretary. His primary obligation is not, however, to his council nor is he appointed by it. It is the national Executive Committee of the Federation which appoints regional secretaries, and to which these officials have a more direct responsibility for their actions as well as the Central Council. In fact the duties of the Regional Secretary are defined in Rule 11 (g) which also states that: The Regional Secretary "shall be under the control of the Central Council, and he shall report to the Head Office each week. He shall be known as the Regional Secretary, and shall also act as the Operatives' Secretary of the Regional Joint Wages Committee."

Of course there are many other duties which the Regional Secretary undertakes and, in an industry like construction, the wide range of them cannot be completely covered by the rules. For example, though trade-union recruitment is normally considered a task to be carried out by the individual organizers of the various affiliated unions, occasional regional campaigns are organized with the NFBTO Regional Secretary acting as the co-ordinator. In particular this type of organizing activity is carried out in relation to local authority staffs and also where large building or civil engineering sites are opened up for such projects as power stations or redevelopment areas.

It has been mentioned that the London Regional Council's constitution is not completely similar to that of regions. It has one specific rule in relation to organization of union membership which states that: "The regional Council shall convene meetings of the organisers operating in the London Region to discuss general questions of organisation, at least once a month."

An Important Link

When one considers that the Regional Secretary not only performs important functions within the Federation sphere but is also the Joint Secretary of the Regional Wages Council it can be seen that he is an important link in the chain of negotiating machinery for the construction industry. Rule 11 (j) states that:

> He is responsible to the Central Council for all negotiations on wages, hours and conditions within his Region, and for all questions of an industrial nature that may from time to time arise.
>
> In cases of industrial dispute the Regional Secretary shall have control. He shall have power to sanction the withdrawal of labour on all questions of payment of other than plain-time rates, and shall report such action forthwith to the Head Office of the Federation.
>
> On other questions involving imminent dispute, he must forthwith report details to the Executive Committee of the Federation.

A good secretary can make a great impact on his region and effectively bring about a high co-ordination of union activity, resulting in benefits for all the affiliated organizations. In particular he should ensure that large sites are adequately controlled and that a responsible Federation steward is elected—Federation steward's credentials being issued from his office—to represent issues to the management which affect all of the trades in general.

On matters affecting individual site level, of course, the local branches of the NFBTO are often brought into the picture. For the:

> Federation Branch is the guardian of the Working Rule Agreement governing the rates of wages and hours and conditions of labour, and of any variation of the Agreement sanctioned by the National Joint Council for the Building Industry applicable to its area.
>
> Any violation of the Working Rules Agreement must be immediately reported to the appropriate Local Employers' Association.

The machinery of the Federation, in fact, is a counterpart to that of the National Federation of Building Trades Employers with provisions at each level for negotiation and conciliation.[4] At national and regional levels the machinery is usually well organized but it has not proved possible, in a number of areas, to establish effective local joint committees. The activities of local Federation branches, where they exist, are also circumscribed to some extent though they do have the opportunity to influence national policy.

For instance, each regional council of the Federation is entitled to send motions for consideration at the NFBTO Annual Conference and also two delegates in addition to the Regional Secretary who attends *ex-officio*. The regional councils usually invite local Federation branches to submit motions on policy to them for consideration, and out of all the motions submitted will choose the ones to go forward to Annual Conference on behalf of the region. As branches also have the power to elect five members to the regional council, representatives to the Annual Conference from the regional councils usually include "grass roots" members from local branches.

[4] The negotiation and conciliation machinery is dealt with more extensively in the chapter dealing with the National Joint Council for the Building Industry.

The formal structure of the Federation can, therefore, be considered adequate to meet the need for democratic decisions within the NFBTO and also for dealing with problems which arise within the industry. But in addition to its formal rules the Federation has rarely failed to take any emergency action which might be necessary to meet the challenge of a rapidly developing industry. The Federation, for instance, took the lead in setting up a Conciliation Committee to deal with demarcation problems which might arise from the introduction of new techniques and materials. And while other industries have frequently been rocked with demarcation disputes the construction industry has remained fairly free from this kind of trouble. One of the major contributory factors to this is undoubtedly the fact that the NFBTO has sorted out demarcation disputes between unions and kept them from exploding into trouble on the sites.

When two or more unions claim the right to use new materials, or operate a new technique (as when the bricklayers clashed with the plumbers and glaziers over who should lay glass blocks), the secretary of the NFBTO convenes a special meeting of the Demarcation Committee at which the unions involved argue their case before other union colleagues (not members of the "litigant" unions) who arbitrate on the matter. The responsibility of the Federated unions in handling their internal disputes in this way has in fact drawn a genuine tribute from the employers. It is perhaps the employers who have most adequately summed up the value of the NFBTO for these and other problems in their evidence to the Royal Commission on Trade Unions and Employers Organizations. Para. 51 of the employers' report to the Commission states that while a comparatively large number of building unions is still in existence: "It has not been the experience of the Employers that this multiplicity of trade unions has by itself protracted the process of collective bargaining or made it more difficult. That this is so is mainly attributable to the effectiveness of the NFBTO as a negotiating instrument."

There is, in fact, no doubt that the unions in the construction industry have realized their maximum potential through the

Federation though a great deal could still be done to make the structure more efficient and rewarding. All has not, however, been "sweetness and light" in the development of the NFBTO and short-sighted union leaders have occasionally viewed any expansion of Federation responsibilities as involving a reduction of their own. There has therefore been some obstruction throughout the years to making the Federation even more efficient. In 1924 the AUBTW even went so far as to secede from the Federation because of the mistaken belief that it could "go it alone" and win a progressive "Builders' Charter" for its members without the support of the other unions. It did not rejoin until 4 years later, by which time it became apparent that it could not achieve its objective single-handed. The ASW has also threatened to secede though, fortunately, it has never carried this threat into effect. At other times there have been other unions which have kicked, perhaps naturally, at the bonds of compromise which are essential if the Federation is to continue its work.

A Major Paradox

One of the major paradoxical attitudes of the unions is that when they meet with membership and financial problems in their own organizations, this frequently results in resentment at meeting their commitments to the Federation. It is a paradox because it should be obvious that strength through unity, as expressed in the Federation, is the best way to offset weakness which might develop in any one affiliated union. It is because some unions do react in this way that the Federation's fortunes fluctuate according to what is happening within each of its affiliates. Of course, some of this is unavoidable. If individual membership of unions falls the Federation is bound to feel the pinch because the total numbers affiliated to it will also drop.

And it is a fact that the unions are generally losing ground. This can be clearly seen in the figures of affiliations to the Federation over the years since 1957. Since that year there has been a slow but consistent fall in total affiliations. An attempt has been made to offset this by increasing affiliation fees but obviously this process is not one that can be continued indefinitely and, even if this financial problem did not arise, there is the fact that it is in the best interest of the unions that they should be able to claim they speak for a reasonably wide and representative number of construction workers.

At the moment it would be unrealistic to claim that this is so. Figures indicate that only a minority of workers are at present organized in their individual unions and affiliated to the NFBTO. In Table 7 the total affiliations from the twenty unions were shown as 417,910 at the end of December 1965 and, though we are dealing primarily with the private contracting side of the industry in this chapter, union membership in the table also included workers in local authorities, government ministries and a small number of men employed in building sections of private firms such as ICI.

Affiliations to the Federation must therefore be compared against the total number of men who are available for recruitment in all of these areas of employment. As the figure for "direct labour" building sections of private firms cannot be definitely ascertained we will omit this class and compare Federation affiliated membership against the total labour force in private contracting and public employment. When we do this it can be seen that affiliated membership shows the depressing downward trend revealed in Table 8.

Obviously the Federation's position will only improve if the affiliated unions are capable of strengthening themselves: not that this implies only one-way traffic. By joint action the unions can strengthen the Federation's efficiency, especially in the regional organization of membership recruitment, greater centralization of research, education and publicity. This in turn means improvements in the Federation's machinery which should help the affiliated organizations. Over the past few years there has been sporadic efforts at doing this. At the Exmouth Annual Conference in 1962, in fact, it was decided that it would be more economic

TABLE 8. TOTAL MEMBERSHIP AFFILIATED TO THE NFBTO COMPARED WITH TOTAL LABOUR FORCE IN THE CONSTRUCTION INDUSTRY

Year	Total membership affiliated to the NFBTO	Total labour force* in private contracting and public employment	Numbers affiliated to NFBTO as % of labour force
Dec. 1957	450,722	1,429,000	31·5
Dec. 1965	417,910	1,491,000	28·0

* The figures were obtained from the Ministry of Public Building and Works.

and efficient if the Federation could centralize research and publicity services, and also organize summer schools at which union members could study problems confronting the industry.

A start was made on this work with the publication of the *Builders' Standard,* a tabloid newspaper which was produced centrally by the Federation and purchased in bulk by the affiliated unions for distribution among their own members. In addition to this the Federation organized two summer schools each year, each of a week's duration at which about fifty lay-members from all the affiliated unions met to hear lecturers deal with the machinery of the industry and other related subjects. Unfortunately this momentum has not been maintained and, in fact, shows some signs of faltering. It would be a tragedy for the Federation and its affiliates if this kind of work were not continued and expanded.

It is an accepted fact that the unions in the construction industry have shown themselves anxious and responsible in facing up to technological developments. By their foresight they have managed to overcome many of the purely industrial problems. They now face, in the growth of the labour-only sub-contractors, and an expansion of the self-employed class of worker, factors which seriously aggravate the already difficult job they have of organizing in such a complex industry as construction. But if they can only show the same understanding and statesmanship in relation to their internal problems, as they have with their industrial ones, there should be no reason why they cannot carry their own organizations and the NFBTO to new heights of efficiency and influence within the industry.

CHAPTER 5

Growth of the Building Employer

The Early Years

In the long history of industrial strife between masters and men it is the union story which has attracted most attention. While their organizations have been constantly analysed, criticized and held up for public inspection the employers' side of the story has been comparatively neglected. There appears to be no full-scale publication which thoroughly examines the various stages through which the building employers have passed on the way to establishing their present regional and local organizations, which are linked effectively at the centre by the National Federation. Yet the builders may have, among all the employers' organizations, one of the most interesting stories to be told.

In fact it has been suggested that as building involved the first large-scale industrial organization in Britain, many centuries ago, the building employer should have emerged as a powerful figure long before his counterparts who arose in manufacturing during the industrial revolution. The holders of this theory, however, misunderstand the way in which these large-scale projects were carried out and financed. The kings, nobles or bishops who provided the wealth for construction of the building never thought of resorting to the kind of contractual system which exists today. Their method, on large-scale projects, was to appoint a "master mason" (himself an employee) who was paid an agreed wage for superintending the project. The client, in fact, hired operatives for these projects on an almost exclusively direct labour basis, and also purchased the materials for them to work.

Where the king was concerned he frequently resorted to a system of impressment by which he simply notified certain authorities that they had to deliver a stated number of men to work on a specific project. Edward III used impressment on a number of occasions and, for the building of Windsor Castle, sent an order in 1359 to certain sheriffs and other dignitaries stating:

> Know that we, trusting in the discretion and loyalty of Master Robert of Gloucester, our mason, have assigned and deputed him to take and arrest as many masons as may be necessary for the erection of our works in our castle of Wyndesore, wherever he can find them, within liberties or without, and to place them in our work aforesaid at our wages and to take and arrest all masons whom he shall find contrary or rebellious in this matter and bring them to the aforesaid castle there to be held in prison until they shall find security to remain at those works according to the instructions of the said Robert on our behalf.[1]

There were also occasions when, with building labour being scarce, the king might use his prerogative of impressment on behalf of some noble or religious dignitary who appealed to him for assistance. It is clear from this state of affairs that there was no place for the building contractor in the medieval years even though large-scale building projects were numerous during that period.

Another reason for the late emergence of the building employer is that the "master craftsman", employing a number of his colleagues, has very largely come from the ranks of the operatives (in building, more than most other industries, this is still the position). To do this requires accumulation of capital and when one thinks of the wealth required to purchase materials and hire labour for building castle, palace or monastery, it is obvious that it was impossible for the ordinary operative to become an employer of labour during this period.

From this summary of the early industry it is equally obvious why greater historical tradition lies with the men rather than the master. Whereas it took time for the master to emerge the operatives were early banded together in conditions which automatically

[1] D. Knoop and G. P. Jones, *The Mediaeval Mason*, p. 244.

led to joint discussions about their working conditions. And though there might be a valid technical difference between a client hiring direct labour, and the employer as we know him today, to the medieval operative the client was still the "boss" against whom they would combine to extract better wages and conditions if they could.

It has been suggested that the building employer first appeared in the sector dealing with repairs and maintenance. While this is probably true of woodworking, and one or two other crafts, direct labour still remained the basis of employment for many men engaged in the repair and maintenance of very large buildings. In addition to the numbers employed by the king, probably the most extensive use of direct labour in this way was by the religious authorities. To maintain the fabric of church or abbey there would often be a masons' lodge supervised by a master mason, or "master of the fabric" as he was sometimes entitled. Controlling the work force including the master mason, and responsible for regulating their wages and conditions on behalf of the church authorities, was the church Chapter.

At York the Chapter extended control over the men in the lodge to an unusual degree by the appointment of a clergyman who was given the role of "supervisor". "We may fairly see in him a medieval anticipation of the modern 'speed boss' and in the conditions which produced him a similarity, in all but scale of operations, to those of modern capitalistic factory industry", wrote Knoop and Jones.[2]

However correct Knoop and Jones were in their assumptions about the "speed boss" character of the supervisor their suggestion of similarity between the lodge's conditions and modern capitalist industry is questionable; especially as it cannot be said even yet that building equates in its operations with modern factory industry. In fact, far from developing along factory-type lines, it is more likely that the next step from the employment of the medieval years was in the direction of a system rather like the self-employed person or labour-only gangs of today.

[2] *The Mediaeval Mason*, pp. 61–62.

For though lack of capital would still be a barrier to an operative becoming a full-scale employer he could, on an appeal from the client paying for the building and wishing to have it completed quickly, forgo day wages and contract to do a piece of work for an agreed price. He might even make arrangements to head a small gang of men prepared to sub-contract their labour in this way. The transition to full employer status was still far from complete, however. And even when there were employers who had soundly established themselves in the industry the client sometimes still purchased the necessary materials.

Assuming the emergence of the employer from the operatives' ranks the late Professor Thorold Rogers has claimed that it meant a more direct and amicable relationship between them than has perhaps existed since. "In the past . . . the relationship of employer and employed was exceedingly direct", he wrote. "Nor do I doubt that it was to this directness that the high remuneration of the artizan was due."[3] His main point that a common identity of interest still lay between master and men, and was the basis for mutual consideration and understanding, was substantiated when they later united to fight the general contracting system when it first appeared in the industry.

A Stimulus to Building

A great stimulus to the growth in numbers of building employers, even though still confined to the craft master basis, was Henry VIII's dissolution of the monasteries. Quite apart from its implications for the building industry it was, as economic historians claim, "the cause of large disturbancies in the economic condition of England". Considered specifically in relation to the building industry it is clear that it had an almost revolutionary impact. The concentrated wealth of the monasteries was taken by Henry and a considerable portion of it distributed widely among his followers. In addition to wealth he also rewarded them with "honours" for their assistance in destroying the monasteries.

[3] Thorold Rogers, *Six Centuries of Work and Wages*, p. 543.

This combination of their new-found wealth and status led to a desire to erect elegant dwellings fitting to their position. The abandonment and destruction of the monasteries also coincidentally provided a great deal of ready-prepared stone which could be used for the new buildings. In addition to this the lodges of workmen which had been previously employed to maintain the fabric of the religious buildings were readily available as a supply of labour.

The effect of all this was to change the face of the industry so that the previous concentration of workers on a relatively few projects now gave way to a more widespread labour force occupied on a much greater variety of work. It was in these circumstances that more and more craftsmen found it possible to establish themselves as employers, and gradually the system of the client utilizing direct labour began to fade. No longer did he automatically appoint a "master" who then controlled the job for him. Increasingly he began to make contracts with employers for a particular job of work to be carried out.

At this stage we should perhaps make clear the distinction which used to exist between the word "master" and "employer". Though they are now almost synonymous that was not always the position. A "master" was once regarded as a master of his particular craft rather than a master of men. He reached the stage of being recognized as a master when he showed himself capable of performing a specially difficult piece of work upon which he proved his craft ability, hence the word "masterpiece". By the time of the religious reformation and its aftermath the word master had come to mean a craftsman trained in a particular craft who employed others of his craft to carry out contracts.

And if the revolution in religion gave rise to a great number of these master craftsmen it was the agricultural and Industrial Revolution at the turn of the eighteenth century which accelerated the trend. As the land Enclosure Acts of this period dispossessed many of the agricultural population, and left them with the sole alternative of seeking a living in the town-based factories, so the building industry found itself with the task of providing both the new factories and the houses in which the workers were to live. This period might well be described as the boom years of the early building industry. More operatives were brought into building and quite large craft master firms began to develop: especially throughout the Midlands and in those areas where the industrial revolution was making its greatest impact.

Not only did the employer class become more soundly established but a "division of labour" began to develop in the responsibilities of the employer. Up to the early part of the nineteenth century the building employer generally designed as well as constructed the dwelling commissioned by his client. Gradually the design function became a special field of its own leading to the birth of a new professional—the architect. The building employer henceforth became limited to the actual construction of the works. This split between the design and construction responsibilities, while no doubt inevitable and to some extent desirable, may have tended to detract from the general efficiency of building operations (a point dealt with at greater length in Chapter 2).

Once the initial impetus of the industrial revolution was exhausted the building industry began to suffer a setback in which the craft masters found it necessary to become tougher over wages and conditions. They also had another and more immediately serious problem confronting them. The Industrial Revolution may have benefited the craft masters in some ways but it also involved the construction of many large and diverse projects for which clients were no longer prepared to go through the tedious business of negotiating contracts with the dozen or more individual craft masters who might be needed. And it was client resentment against the old contractual system which led inevitably to the birth of the general contractor who undertook the control and management of the entire project.

The craft masters had no doubts where this trend would lead if unresisted: their own gradual elimination. They successfully persuaded their operatives that such a change would destroy the close link which had existed between craft master and men and that the general contractor would bring about a worsening of working conditions. And (as more fully explained in Chapter 3) in the early 1830's they forgot their own acrimonious quarrels— like brothers engaged in a fight—and turned with unanimity on the "intruder" and common enemy the general contractor.

Though they attempted to "black" all jobs done under general contract it was obvious that their campaign was doomed to failure. But the solidarity displayed by the unions at this time demonstrated to the employers how sadly lacking their organization was by comparison and how badly placed they were should a dispute break out. These apprehensions were fully realized when, just a short time after the abortive campaign against the general contractor, the operatives peremptorily presented their employers with a list of demands of wages and conditions. In Liverpool they also added insult to injury by the way in which they presented their demands. "We consider", they wrote to the employers, "that you have not treated our rules with the deference you ought to have done, we consider you highly culpable and deserving of being severely chastised."

The employers were outraged by the demands and also the way in which the various trade unions, organized together in the Operative Builders' Union, presented them. Therefore in 1833, at a hastily summoned meeting, they decided to take up the challenge which had been flung at them. And though they undoubtedly won the lengthy and bitter dispute which followed, the main lesson of the conflict—that they required to maintain organized contact with each other—was apparently not learned. Any form of association which they had with each other was still on a very tentative basis and confined within craft lines. On the other hand, the unions were not only more firmly organized within their trades but had shown, in the attempt at federation through the Operative Builders' Union, that they were prepared to cross trade boundaries if this provided them with a more effective organization.

Looked at objectively the situation was really what might have been expected. The operatives, working together in a yard or on a site with their working conditions as a common point of interest, obviously found it easier to create organizations in these circumstances. The employers were in a very different situation. Their basic relationship with one another was one of competition not co-operation. They might meet occasionally to discuss trade prospects but the founding of formal organizations was not viewed with the same enthusiasm as it was among the operatives.[4]

The associations of employers which sprang sporadically into existence did so in response to trade union pressures rather than a positive desire to build stable organizations for long-term purposes. They associated together for so long as a challenge had to be met then they faded into inactivity again. The 1833 full-blooded battle against the Operative Builders' Union was a case in point. Although the employers in Liverpool could have seized that opportunity for maintaining and improving the united organization they had then, they allowed it to drift after the crisis was over and it was not until 33 years later, in an area renowned for bitter disputes between masters and men, that there was formed a permanent Liverpool Federation of Employers.

It is the unions in fact which can, paradoxically, claim to have been responsible for providing the impetus towards creating the employers' organizations! Wherever the unions were strongest the employers found themselves forced into "banding together . . . for the purpose of mutual protection against the demands of the Unions".[5] So it was that when the Operative Builders' Union collapsed, and with it the union hopes of a federal organization, it appears that the operatives and employers retreated to their individual craft structures.

---

[4] The kind of fierce competition which could exist between employers – as distinct from between employers and men – is clearly revealed in the *Ragged Trousered Philanthropists* by Robert Tressell. This famous book was written by an operative who wanted to portray the miseries of workmen but still had an objective eye with which to view the tragedy of employers who became "victims of the system".

[5] *A Brief History of the North Western Federation of Building Trade Employers.*

And it was along craft lines that, throughout the country and especially in the Midlands and London, there gradually evolved a system of local negotiations to establish the particular wages and conditions applying to the various trades. The serious drawback to this form of negotiation, from the employers' point of view, was that while they were limited organizationally to their local associations the union branches they negotiated with usually had the advice and support of their national bodies.

The Midlands Strike

As the nineteenth century progressed the employers began to enlarge the scope of their associations from local to district level, and a few visionaries had their eyes set on an even more widely based structure. They reasoned that union demands were now becoming uniform and national in character: a national employers' association was best fitted to answer the challenge. In particular the operatives were making a determined attempt to shorten the working day.

The first move was made by the London operatives who approached their national union committees and asked for official backing for a strike to get hours reduced to nine a day. The response they had was less than enthusiastic. The national committees were sceptical of the ability of the London branches to win the shorter working day—and were also short of funds. They therefore said that they would be unable to give financial aid should a strike break out. When the operatives failed to get national backing for a strike they decided on the more peaceful alternative of petitioning the employers to declare a half day on Saturday. But by this time the London employers had become strongly organized and were confident of being able to resist any challenge from the operatives. In addition they were fully aware that the national union committees had turned a deaf ear to the plea for financial aid and consequently the position of the London operatives was weak. They therefore rejected the petitions out of hand and there the matter rested—at least for some time.

The men in the Midlands area were not prepared to let the "great objective" stagnate, however, and when they subsequently began to agitate for a shorter working day the Midlands employers knew that a bitter battle was likely to be the final outcome. For the employers fully realized that in the Midlands "storm centre" they were facing a more determined body of men who would probably not hesitate to strike for their objectives, even if it meant being without official union backing or dispute benefit. This apprehension by the employers, and a belief that any conflict over hours could be very widespread, led them to take the precautionary step of forming the National Association of Master Builders at the beginning of 1858. At the beginning it was confined mainly to the Midlands and the North where it was thought the struggle might be fiercest.

The peculiar fact about the formation of the National Association—probably a forerunner of the present National Federation of Building Trades Employers—is that little mention is made of it in published histories. It is in the records of the Operative Stonemasons' Union, which anxiously watched this step being taken by the masters, that we gain information about its growth. "The movement commenced at Liverpool", reported the Masons' General Secretary to his members, "and meetings have been held in various large towns throughout the Kingdom. The Liverpool masters consulted those of Manchester and the result was that they resolved to send delegates to various towns. This has been done, and associations have been formed in Bolton, Halifax, Nottingham, Birmingham, Sheffield and Huddersfield."[6]

There is no doubt that this attempt at national federation was the most ambitious which had been made by the employers. And so confident did they become at the speed with which employers joined the Association that it was decided to forestall the operatives by precipitating the battle themselves. This they did

[6] OSM Returns, 29 April 1858 (now in the possession of the Amalgamated Union of Building Trade Workers).

by informing the operatives that they intended introducing a system of payment by the hour instead of the traditional day wage. The employer's announcement certainly had an immediate effect, for the unions regarded it as the greatest threat they had ever faced. In fact the great hostility and unity which the proposal created caused the employers to become apprehensive about the possible issue of the dispute. Too late they saw that they had overplayed what originally looked a strong hand by attacking a principle the unions held to be the very basis of reasonable working conditions.

The unions therefore regarded the dispute as one which had to be climaxed by victory at all costs. "Prepare for a determined resistance against the introduction of this hour system", wrote Harnott of the Operative Stonemasons, "and then you will be serving yourselves, and confer a blessing on the offspring who succeed you."

Faced with this spirit the hastily thrown up association of employers could not win and, in fact, found itself broken within a very short time. The dispute began on 1 May 1858, and only a few days later the employers in the towns connected with the National Association of Master Builders had all given way except for those in Huddersfield and Newcastle. Even though the employers in these two towns offered greater resistance they too conceded by 17 May. And with this defeat the National Association of Master Builders appears to have temporarily collapsed as an effective organization.

To a great extent their defeat and disintegration was due to the way in which they had approached the conflict. Though they had achieved considerable success in getting employers to join their National Association the primary motive was again a panic reaction to the expected dispute with the operatives. The Association had, in addition, so little time to consolidate itself before the dispute that it could not really present a formidable front to unions absolutely united in their antagonism to payment by the hour. The fact that the National Association also disintegrated after their defeat shows too that their attitude towards co-operative activity among employers had not matured beyond questions of defence against immediate threats from the unions.

The Midlands and Northern employers were not the only ones apparently reluctant to found permanent associations, even in the face of events proving them to be necessary. The London masters also failed to profit by their experiences a year later when they also entered a dispute over payment by the hour. In London the position remained much the same as before the Midlands and Northern battle took place. The central committees of the unions were still refusing official strike backing for an "hours dispute" so the men had continued with their policy of presenting petitions —which the employers continued to reject.

In the summer of 1859 the operatives decided to approach a further four firms which they chose, by ballot, to petition for the 9-hour day. When approached by the delegation one firm reacted by sacking the masons who had taken a leading part in presenting the petition. Up to this action the petitioning had been a reasonably peaceful exercise but now the rest of the operatives employed by the firm immediately came out on strike in protest. In other London firms both employers and men realized that the "peace" was now over and they waited tensely for the widespread explosion which they knew was now almost inevitable.

In facing up to the prospects of such a dispute the London masters, though still not organized on a regional basis, nevertheless knew they had very strong links with each other compared to other regions. Therefore, on the theory that the first to land a blow usually wins the fight, they decided to forestall the inevitable strike for a shorter working week by declaring a lock-out. On 6 August 1859 they made the lock-out effective and threw a total of nearly 25,000 men out on the streets.

After the lock-out had gone on for 6 weeks the employers decided that the operatives were now sufficiently chastened and would be in no position to engage in a strike for the 9-hour day. They therefore announced that their yards would now be opened to workmen—with the qualification that they must first sign a document declaring non-membership of a trade union. Though

I.R.C.—D

a number of men were prepared to do this in order to resume work, the "document" qualification met with determined resistance from many of the stronger unions and 6 months dragged by before it was finally decided by the employers to withdraw the document because: "The objects contemplated by the declaration having been accomplished, its further formal administration is unnecessary."

Certainly this was largely true and the London employers had demonstrated a remarkable degree of solidarity which had enabled them to present an effective opposition to the unions. This solidarity they retained to the extent that, when the operatives again resorted to petitioning for the 9-hour day in 1861, the employers once more effectively delivered a counter-stroke. In response to the petition from the operatives they announced that they proposed to introduce payment by the hour. This was the shrewd move which the Midland and Northern Employers had earlier attempted. The employer's reasoning was simple and sound. Day wages still applied in the industry and to cut hours from 10 to 9 a day, with the same daily rate being paid, was equal to increasing the rate per hour. But payment by the hour would mean that a reduction in working hours would automatically involve a reduction in wages. This, they thought, was a certain way of curing the men's desire for a shorter working day!

Led by the firms of Kelk, Lucas, Smith and Axford they therefore informed the operatives that, as from the 23 March 1861, "day wages would stop and be supplanted by payment at the rate of 7d. per hour". It was this announcement which sparked off one of the most epic battles between employers and operatives ever seen in London. Though during the struggle there were employers who conceded and retained day wages, and operatives who gave in and went to work for payment by the hour, many employers and men were in dispute for over a year on this fundamental principle.

When the fight was over, however, it was obvious that the majority of men in London had accepted the new hourly system and gradually it became widespread throughout the whole country.

And in this major victory the employers had shown that, by demonstrating the same unity which had animated the unions during their early struggles, they could achieve success. It seems incredible, therefore, that they did not follow up this advantage by establishing a permanent regional federation as a consequence of this particular experience. It was not until 10 years later, in fact, that London Masters took this essential step.

By that time the next move towards national federation had already taken place and again Liverpool was the area which revived the concept. Their National Association of Master Builders had lain dormant since the defeat of the Midland and Northern employers during the first major strike over payment by the hour. In 1865, however, it was formally revived and a General Builders' Association was established with a definite constitution.

The first moves had, in fact, been taken a year earlier when the employers in the Midland Counties had decided to form an association. The 1865 meeting of the General Builders' Association, held in August at the Royal Hotel in Birmingham, was able to record, however, that the Association was now organized on a widespread basis with thirty-six associations affiliated in both England and Scotland (though the London Employers were not attached to it). Even more important was the statement by the Chairman of the meeting, Mr. Lovatt of Wolverhampton, that there was full recognition of past mistakes which had led to organizational failure.

He particularly castigated previous short-sighted attempts at 'Association upon some one fundamental idea or rule rather than upon the common interest of the trade". Looking beyond mere industrial protection as a sufficient purpose for holding the Association together he spoke of establishing general trade practises; setting down the type of relationship which should exist between architect and builder; the publication of a trade newspaper and the particular objective "of conveying to every member reliable trade intelligence and information of every character". He did not ignore the fact, however, that protection against strikes was a prime purpose of the Association and that lack of organization in the past had often led to defeat. "The manner in which strikes had been and are carried on is such as to almost ensure success to the trade unions as opposed to disunited Masters and for want of organization we have been content, perforce, to idly watch the struggle and to know that we are indirectly assisting the enemy while the fight was not at our own doors and to suffer for it or helplessly yield when it came there."[7]

Though Lovatt had set down the general principles upon which the Association might be organized on a stable basis the General Builders' Association did not meet with the success anticipated and, in 1868, the employers interested in building a permanent and widespread organization held a further meeting in Liverpool to discuss basic proposals for regulating wages and conditions which would apply throughout the country.[8] Among the employers present were probably some of those who had been adherents of the national federation idea since the foundation of the first association in 1858. In particular it was given strong support by the Liverpool employers who had given concrete evidence of their desire for unity among masters by establishing the Liverpool Master Builders' Association on 1 October 1866. In this they had given a lead to the other areas.

Few other areas or regions were as advanced in their thinking. In fact, with the exception of London, the Southern, Eastern and Western parts of the country did not have any form of regional federation until the first 20 years of this century. And even in London, the other major battleground of the industry apart from Liverpool, it was not until 1872 that the London Master Builders Association was formed.

From about 1875, however, there was a gradual growth in local associations and a consequent evolution towards regional identity. The reason for expansion in employers' organizations

[7] From Minute Book of the General Builders' Association now in the possession of the National Federation of Building Trades Employers.

[8] See *The Builder* report in issue of 24 October 1868.

during this particular period was that general economic conditions were turning in their favour contrasted with the few years previously when, from 1870 onwards, general economic and political conditions had favoured the unions. With a heavy demand for labour they had been able to improve wages and conditions and simultaneously achieve changes in the law which gave them the "legality" which they had been fighting for over the past 47 years.[9] This greater prosperity for the unions, and the consequent strengthening of their national organizations, drove home some basic lessons to the employers and they became more than ready to improve their associations with one another when circumstances changed in their favour. All their previous struggles towards national unity finally came to fruition in 1878 with the creation of the National Association of Master Builders of Great Britain. The formation of this Association was the turning-point for the employers because, though it passed through the kind of crisis which had afflicted earlier attempts at national federation, it did not, like them, disintegrate. It provided a continuing lifeline through to the present-day NFBTE.

The successful creation of the National Association was also of considerable importance in its impact on the relationship between the employers and operatives. From now on the employers were in the stronger position for the unions, though they had been making progress with their individual national trade organizations, had still not succeeded in establishing a federation to provide the kind of effective link which the National Association of Master Builders gave to the employers.

The National Association's birth also coincided with a downturn in the country's economic position and, as a result, the power of the unions to enforce claims for improvement in conditions was considerably weakened in any case. As this trade depression

[9] Although it was no longer illegal to form unions after the repeal of the Anti-Combinations Acts in 1824, the unions had retained the taint of "illegality" because they were held to be in "restraint of trade". It was not until the Trade Union Act of 1871, therefore, that they were given the formal legal status which enabled them to seek protection of the law for their property and funds.

worsened the employers announced that wage rates would have to be cut. And now it was the turn of the unions to panic into action at the threat of the superior organization ranged against them. At a hastily summoned meeting on 27 February 1879, delegates from various building unions met in London and resolved: "This meeting believes that, in view of the aggressiveness shown by the National Federation of Employers, it is desirable to form a National Federation of Building Operatives."

This would certainly have been a wise move but, irrespective of the adventurous mood of this meeting, another 39 years elapsed before they followed the example of the employers and formed a national federation. What is significant about the 1879 union meeting, however, is that the titles used to identify the organizations are similar to the ones in use today although it was some years before the employers formally changed the name of their federation to the National Federation of Building Trade Employers. In fact it transformed itself from the National Association of Master Builders of Great Britain to the National Association of Master Builders of Great Britain and Ireland before officially becoming the NFBTE in 1899.

The Federation Strengthens

During the 69 years which have elapsed since the formal adoption of this title the most ironical fact is that the Liverpool employers, who did so much to foster the idea of national federation, were isolated from it for a total period of 22 years. From 1920–3 and 1926–42 the Liverpool employers were disaffiliated and in a wilderness not entirely of their own making.

To a great extent the reason for the course they had taken lay in the operatives' insistence on negotiating wages and conditions on a Liverpool basis rather then accept the national agreement which was established after the end of the First World War. This was because they could, with their militant tradition and effective unity, secure better conditions for themselves than other operatives could enforce throughout the country as a whole.

In fact the woodworkers and the bricklayers, the two most powerful unions in the building industry, reported in 1919 that the highest wage rates they were able to obtain were in the Liverpool area. In addition to this aspect the question of personal differences within the employers ranks coloured the situation somewhat.

A further aggravation of the problem was the aftermath of the national strike which took place within the industry in 1924. One of the main issues involved in the dispute (as more fully explained in Chapter 3) was an insistence by the National Federation of Building Trade Employers that the unions should make the Liverpool members toe the line where the National Working Rules were concerned. When the strike was settled this issue was still unsatisfactorily resolved and the position did not ease as far as the Liverpool employers were concerned. But it was still some time before they fully appreciated that remaining outside the National Federation placed them at a serious disadvantage when facing the united and militant operatives. And even when they rejoined the NFBTE in 1942 there still remained 3 years of delicate negotiating before the Liverpool area finally came to accept the National Working Rules laid down by the National Joint Council for the Building Industry. One condition of acceptance being that the Liverpool operatives received the same special wage rate as applied in the London area.

With the reaffiliation of the Liverpool area in 1942, and the affiliation of the Scottish Federation of Building Trade Employers in 1963, the NFBTE has now successfully established nation-wide links upon which it has developed its activities and services to become one of the most effective employers' organizations in Britain today.

CHAPTER 6

The National Federation of Building Trade Employers

The First Functions

Though the National Federation of Building Trade Employers can trace its direct origins back to the creation of the National Association of Master Builders in 1878 it was not until 1906 that the first full-time General Secretary was appointed. Previously the Federation's work had been carried out by a part-time secretary. This late appointment of a full-time secretary with an adequate staff to service him, signifies one of the major historical differences between the NFBTE and that of its counterpart in the industry—the National Federation of Building Trades Operatives. When the NFBTO was formed in 1918 it was immediately endowed with full-time personnel. As the bodies directly represented on the NFBTO were the national executives of the affiliated unions it meant that the Federation's structure was, and still is, designed and applied from the top.

With the NFBTE the pattern was reversed. Local and regional organizations of employers were in existence in many areas for a considerable time before the central association was created. The pre-existence of the local organizations is logically explained by the fact that all labour negotiations, and most other matters of importance, were handled locally. Therefore, the early importance of the national body's role was in providing a co-ordinating and advisory service. It was not necessary, however, for it to give the all-round assistance on negotiations which would obviously have involved the appointment of full-time staff.

When the structure was finally consolidated in 1906 it was partially symbolic of a gradual change in the outlook of the affiliated members and also of changing national circumstances. It was not only that the local and regional organizations recognized the increasing need for centralized negotiations and general advice on major industrial matters, but also their view of the national role to be played by the NFBTE had considerably widened. Firstly, in such a complex industry as building, the central agency of the employers, they reasoned, could provide service and information on commercial and other matters in addition to those more directly connected with industrial relations. Secondly, with the coming into power of the Campbell-Bannerman Government and its avowed intention of carrying out a radical programme, the NFBTE decided to consolidate and expand its organization to fulfil any demands which might consequently be made upon it. The head office, at first situated in Liverpool and then Manchester, was transferred to London and Mr. A. G. White was appointed in 1906 as the first full-time General Secretary.

White was one of those grand characters—which the building industry flings up quite frequently—who had a thorough knowledge of the industry, allied to an understanding of the union viewpoint, and this combination of virtues enabled him to establish the NFBTE on a sound basis whilst preserving good industrial relations. His stamina was certainly undoubted for he remained General Secretary until he died at the age of 90, during the Second World War, while on his way home from a meeting of the National Joint Council for the Building Industry. To White is credited the foundation of an industrial relations policy that the employers, and the officials of its Federation, must always try "to play fair". When the NFBTE further expanded its organization by appointing Sir Jonah Walker-Smith its first Director in 1924, he adopted the general basis of White's principles in addition to insisting upon the need for a consistent long-term policy for the industry and for efficient conduct of all NFBTE business.

Because of this multi-purpose role, which has become increasingly evident in recent years, the Federation's legal status is that of an unregistered trade union. It is not only an employers' organization dealing with labour relations but also a trade organization occupied with commercial matters. It justifiably prides itself on dealing with a wide range of matters affecting all spheres of the industry while emphasizing that no attempt is made to control the trading activities of its members. Though questions concerning industrial relations receive more publicity, the other activities indulged in by the NFBTE are worth some examination. In fact a diagram attempting to show all the interests of the Federation would appear almost as intricate as a spider's web. Apart from the detailed structure of the NFBTE itself, there are a large number of organizations affiliated to it and also a considerable amount of interlocking functions with other bodies. Figure 4 (prepared by officials of the NFBTE) gives some idea of the range of Federation activities.

Though we cannot describe them all here, two significant activities, in which the Federation has been a prime mover, are the creation of the National House Builders Registration Council (NHBRC) and the Advisory Service for the Building Industry. Though the NHBRC is now firmly established as an independent body, with representation on its Council from a wide variety of national organizations and also given the official blessing of the government, it must be acknowledged that its formation in 1936 was due to the far-sighted initiative of the NFBTE. The Advisory Service was established at a later date by the Federation—in 1954—to fill a very great vacuum in the industry; that of collecting and disseminating advice to individual firms on problems of management.

Run as a non-profit-making concern the Advisory Service is of great value to members of the NFBTE. The Federation has also shown initiative by not limiting the service to members alone and it is open to any firm enterprising enough to take the opportunity of utilizing it. Though these two examples of the Federations' general activities are particularly indicative of its

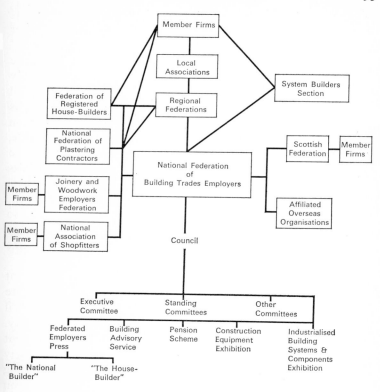

FIG. 4. Organization of the National Federation of Building Trade
Employers.

wide range they reveal only a small part of this kind of work.
One fact which clearly reveals the importance of the standing
of the Federation in this direction is that around twenty overseas
countries are affiliated for the purpose of interchanging literature
and information. Perhaps even more indicative is that the full
range of objects set out in the Constitution and Rules of the
NFBTE is a very long one indeed—running from A to S. Some,

of course, are peripheral activities compared to others. The Federation itself regards the seven most important objects as being:

(a) To agree, and secure general observance of, fair and equitable rates of wages and conditions of employment, and to ensure peace in the industry, thus protecting members against loss arising from industrial disputes.

(b) To agree and establish fair and equitable standard forms and conditions of tendering, contracting and trading.

(c) To encourage and promote education and training (including apprenticeship).

(d) To encourage building research and the dissemination of technical information.

(e) To represent the views of building trades employers to government departments, local authorities, public, professional and other bodies, including manufacturers and merchants of building materials.

(f) To protect the interests of members in relation to legislation and litigation.

(g) To improve the status of the building employers and the standards of construction.

Though it is sometimes alleged that the NFBTE mainly represents the interests of the large general contractor its membership category, to the contrary, is very wide. Any firm which employs labour is eligible for membership, whether they be general contractors, sub-contractors, master plumbers, painters or employers of other crafts. The democratic foundations of the Federation are therefore well established. With the technological developments that have been taking place in the industry there has also been an increasing awareness of the need for providing a forum for specialized interests. The Federation organization is therefore being gradually supplemented, as opportunity offers, by developing the affiliation of specialist groups such as house-builders, shop-fitters, etc., which represent the particular interests of different sections of the industry.

All members, in whatever section of the industry, also have full rights and status under the Constitution and Rules. In addition they are entitled to stand for any office within the Federation or for election to its top governing Council. This Council exercises control over the Federation's policy and administration. On the Council the regional federations—as might be expected from the historical tradition and background of the NFBTE—have a very strong influence. In fact the present ninety-five-member council has sixty-three regional representatives on it, together with fourteen representatives of affiliated bodies, and eighteen seats allocated to *ex-officio* and co-opted members.

With this very strong "ground roots" representation from almost self-contained regions it might be inferred that the central control and authority of the NFBTE is less than that in the nationally dominated operatives' Federation. In fact, this is not so. In practice both federations face much the same complications in obtaining compromise leading to agreement among members and have equal standing within their respective fields. On wage claims, for example, each side has to take "soundings" of what will prove acceptable to the majority of its affiliates. The operatives' side will hold out against accepting a lower offer than it thinks union membership will tolerate, while the employers' Federation cannot nationally agree to a figure which is so high that it is likely to cause mutiny among its members.

The situation, in essence, resolves itself into what might be called a clash of democratic opinion between both sides! Finally the leaders of both federations have to use their "soundings" as the basis around which they thrash out a reasonable compromise aimed at enabling the industry to get on with its job with all parties getting a reasonable financial reward for their efforts. Given this basic fact of the sensitivity of both federations to local and regional pressures, it is probably true that the Council of the NFBTE can sometimes show a more united front than the operatives' Federation. This may be partially due to the fact that, with the identity of interest the employers have in relation to the general commercial activities of their Federation, they are able to reach agreement more amicably on the line to be taken during industrial negotiations.

Council of the Federation

The Council of the NFBTE, which meets monthly, is itself given broad policy guidance by the General Meeting of members. The Council, however, remains the effective governing body of the NFBTE and is under no obligation to implement the views of the General Meeting (the relationship is in some ways similar to that of certain trade unions where the executives hold ultimate power but find annual delegate conferences useful for collecting the views of ordinary members). The Rules provide for at least two General Meetings to take place each year. The Annual General Meeting "shall be held not later than the 14th day of February in each year" while the Half-yearly General (or Summer) Meeting is scheduled to be held in either May, June or July.

The A.G.M. is, of course, the more important as it is at this meeting that the election of officers takes place, the Annual Report of the Council is presented and the accounts examined. Nevertheless, the Summer meeting has, in the past few years, become more significant because it is now followed by a conference at which top-ranking speakers are invited to give lectures on matters of topical interest.

What may be a unique feature of the Constitution and Rules of the NFBTE is that they allow the right of every individual member to attend General Meetings. Of course, the great majority of members do not take advantage of this rule or it would quickly become inoperative! Attendances at General Meetings have a rather wide variation with anything between 200 and 500 members turning up. When voting takes place on resolutions the decision is usually made by a show of hands. If a poll vote is requested, however, then only accredited representatives of Regions and

Associations (the numbers of such depending on subscriptions paid by them in the preceding year) are entitled to vote.

The officers elected at the Annual General Meeting number five. They are the President, Senior Vice-President, First Junior Vice-President, Second Junior Vice-President and the Treasurer. These officers are subject to annual election. In effect what happens is that the three vice-presidents move up one grade—as the President retires—and a new Second Junior Vice-President is elected at the A.G.M.

In addition to the elected officers two others are appointed as Federation officers for the year. These are the immediate past-president of the Federation, and the Chairman of the National Joint Council for the Building Industry if he is a member of the NFBTE. These two appointments are valuable in that one provides for continuity among the Council's officers while the other gives a direct link between the Federation and the official industrial relations machinery.

With the many interests and activities of the NFBTE the six meetings of the Council which are held per year would not be able to exercise detailed control over its activities, however, and six Standing Committees are elected each year for specific duties. These are:

(i) Finance Committee.
(ii) Defence Committee.
(iii) Wages and Conditions Committee.
(iv) Contracts Committee.
(v) Membership Committee.
(vi) Public Relations Committee.

The Executive Committee

These committees are in addition to the Executive Committee of the Federation, which is the most important of those appointed for it is given full powers to act on urgent matters between meetings of the full Council. Because it has such vital functions, and its decisions have to be widely accepted, the composition of the Executive is very carefully balanced. In addition to the officers of the NFBTE each regional federation has a representative on the Executive and there is also one representative from the Scottish Federation of Employers and one from the House Builders Federation.

The full range of the Federation's services also requires the appointment of other committees and frequently necessitates the setting up of special committees to examine questions which do not fall within the purview of the committees established according to the Rules and Constitution. Another indication of the wide ranging interests of the Federation can be seen from the fact that there is a total of sixty staff at head office: this is more full-time personnel than the aggregate head office and regional staff of the Operatives' Federation—which is nevertheless accepted as the most extensive union federal organization in the country.

The administration of the NFBTE is in the hands of a Director who is provided with a Deputy Director to assist him. In addition there are senior officers responsible for a large number of important departments including industrial relations, legal advice, education and training, and accident prevention.

This head office staff is further supplemented by the full-time personnel in each of the affiliated regional federations. In fact, even some of the local associations within the regions employ their own full or part-time local association secretaries. Usually the part-time secretaries are professional men in private practice.

However, there is a gradual trend towards an extension of the principle of regional control of administration throughout the whole of their territory, with administrative work being undertaken by the full-time regional staff. The growing popularity of this system is due to the feeling that this is the road to a more efficient and extensive service to members. And there is also the fact that staff employed full-time dealing with the Federation's affairs will be more closely in touch with national policy and activities than part-time secretaries who, naturally enough, do not regard the affairs of the building industry as other than a branch of their private practices.

Having an experienced staff is of particular importance to regional and local associations because their function is directly related to the needs of the individual member. They help him in dealing with his particular problems and only refer to the national head office on cases involving more difficult contractual or labour matters. The regional and local associations remain, of course, subject to the control of the National Federation on the vital issues which involve national agreements, policies or administration. There are ten regional federations in England and Wales affiliated to the NFBTE and these cover the areas of Liverpool, Yorkshire, South Wales, Southern Counties, London, Northern Counties, North-Western, South-Western, Midland and Eastern.[1] These regions have area boundaries which are similar to the regions set up by the National Federation of Building Trades Operatives and, in fact, co-operate with the operatives' regional councils in establishing the joint regional negotiating machinery.

However, the regional federations affiliated to the NFBTE are not hand-maidens to their national Council to the same extent as those of the NFBTO. In setting down the actual Rules and Constitution of the regional and local associations they are, in reasonable measure, left to their own discretion except that certain essential national rules must be incorporated.

The local associations which are grouped within the regions— excepting the London and Liverpool regions which have none— total about 260. These associations are of particular importance within the structure of the NFBTE because it is at this level that most employer members take part in the democratic process of the Federation. Application for membership, however, can be made either to the regional federation or to the local association covering the area in which the applicant's head office is situated.

[1] The Scottish Employers' Federation is also affiliated for all matters except those in respect of which Scottish law and practice differ from English law and practice.

Because of the measure of autonomy within local associations and regional federations, applicants for membership have to sign a form indicating that the application is being made simultaneously for membership of the appropriate local or regional organization and of the National Federation. The applicant also agrees to abide by the sets of rules applying to all levels of the NFBTE.

One class strictly prohibited from joining the NFBTE is any person belonging to a trade union! To those who do not know the industry this might seem a remote possibility in any event but many operatives do, in fact, become employers and therefore have to make a choice of whether or not to resign from trade-union membership to join the NFBTE. In certain cases exemption may be granted. The membership strength of the associations within any one region determines the influence that region can exercise, through its representatives, on the national policies adopted by the NFBTE. And to ensure accurate registration at head office level a return of membership, including the size of their affiliation, is to be made on or before the 24th day of March in each year.

Income and Expenditure

The "size of affiliation" is particularly important because it is not the number of members which effectively counts but the size of the enterprises which they control. The basis of subscription to the National Federation, in fact, is on the amount of wages paid by each member during the previous financial year. As representation on the National Council is proportionate to the total amount of wage-related subscriptions, then regions with the larger employer power have accordingly a greater influence on Federation policy.

The actual amount of national affiliation fee paid, the standard rate, is 1s. 7d. per £100 of wages and salaries paid by employer members. To ensure equity of payment for services received a sliding scale of affiliation fees operates. Under this the members pay a reduced rate of subscriptions on that part of their wages return which comes above a prescribed figure. On the other hand, the minimum amount upon which a member can affiliate is equal to a "wages paid" figure of £525 in the previous financial year (it should be noted that these fees are for the National Federation and, in addition, regional and local subscriptions must also be paid).

The standard rate of 1s. 7d. per £100 of wages paid has remained at this level since 1956. In fact it is a reduction on the rate which applied just after the war when it equalled 2s. for each £100 of wages paid. When this is contrasted with the frequent financial crises in the operatives' federation it would appear, at first glance, as if the NFBTE had achieved something remarkably like a financial miracle. The significant difference is, however, that the NFBTO affiliates do so on a *per capita* payment while the employers' federation, basing its fees on the amount paid in wages, finds that inflation results in an increase in fees paid.

As wages have risen in the industry so membership subscriptions to the NFBTE have automatically risen. Since 1956 the basic hourly rate in building has gone up by over 60 per cent. This is not the complete picture for total earnings paid out to operatives have risen, through overtime and incentives, by nearly 20 per cent more than basic rates. Therefore, without having to change their subscription rule the income of the NFBTE may have increased by nearly 80 per cent since 1956.

This figure does not, of course, take into consideration any net increase in membership of the Federation during those years. And though accurate statistics of membership are not available the NFBTE calculates that:

> Virtually all the larger building firms in the country, i.e. firms employing over 250 men, are members of the Federation and 60 per cent of the medium-sized firms, i.e. those employing 100-250 men. The percentage of membership diminishes with the size of firm, but numerically the largest number of members fall in the size group employing 20 men or less. It is estimated that of the total labour force employed by contractors, the proportion employed by firms in membership with the Federation is over 60 per cent.

There is also the fact that the total size of the labour force within the construction industry has been increasing. The NFBTE itself estimates that: "Due to the increased volume of building work and the general inflation, the income of the Federation has quadrupled since 1946." This is only one-half of the story, however. What inflation gives it can also take away. Salaries and general administrative costs, for example, have risen to match the rise in income. Affiliation fees to other organizations have also increased, such as the National Joint Council for the Building Industry whose administrative machine is financed jointly by the employers and the unions.

When one considers that the NFBTE has also considerably extended its services to members in the last few years it is obvious that even built-in rises in income are not sufficient to allow for the expansion which is necessary in services. There are years, in fact, when the Federation has to draw on reserves to meet deficits arising on annual income. In the face of these facts there may therefore be a danger that, while developments in the construction industry require an extension of the activities of the NFBTE, its income may gradually begin to fall off relevant to its commitments. To some extent the Council of the Federation recognizes that present finances do not allow it to carry out all the work it would like to do. In its evidence to the Royal Commission on Trade Unions and Employers Associations, the National Federation wistfully remarks:

> There are a number of directions in which, if additional funds were available, the Federation could do even more useful work for the benefit of the industry, e.g. in the development of research into technical processes, in the wider dissemination of technical and economic information, in the promotion of recruitment to the industry, in greater propaganda for safety, in the preparation of a register of qualified builders, etc.

But like the unions the NFBTE has to look at the other side of the coin. When considering the consequences of extending these services the Council's evidence concludes:

> It is necessary to balance the value of additional services in the eyes of members with the increased costs which must be met in providing them. Although the amount of subscription now payable by members is, generally speaking, far lower in relation to turnover than it was before the war, there is always the underlying fear in a voluntary organization that any increase in the rate would result in resignations from membership.

In addition to the fees due to the National Federation the employer member has to pay those required by his regional and local association. Resting upon him, therefore, is the financial responsibility of paying for the national, regional and local levels of the organization. This responsibility may vary, however, because local associations have the power to determine the total rate of subscription due—always bearing in mind that the basic wage-related national subscription must be included. It has been estimated that the annual expenditure of the National Federation is around £250,000, and that the addition of regional and local expenditure would probably increase that figure to a total annual expenditure by all levels of the NFBTE to between £500,000–£750,000. This is a large sum to raise and some regional and local associations manage to increment finances through the commission earned on collective insurance schemes which they provide as a service to their members.

This is a classic example of the way in which the actual extension of Federation services can help to increase income. It may be that one way of meeting the growing challenge of the financial problem lies in enlarging developments in this direction. To some extent the publications of the National Federation play a part in this. *The National Builder* and *The House-Builder and Estate Developer* are excellently produced publications (actually published by the Federated Employers Press Ltd., the shares in which are owned by the NFBTE) which do a good public relations job for the Federation in addition to attracting a sizeable amount of advertising revenue. The total income from copy sales is not so great as some people assume, however, because each member of the NFBTE is given a free copy of each publication.

Assisting Industrial Development

Throughout the years since White and Walker-Smith first established the basic foundations of the NFBTE functions and policy there has been a continuing attempt to encourage developments beneficial to the industry as a whole. Since the end of the

Second World War the Federation has faced up to its responsibilities, in this direction, within an industry radically affected by the rapid introduction of new techniques and materials. As almost every section of the industry felt the impact of these changes the NFBTE responded by helping the creation, within its central organization, of specialist groups to deal with developments affecting particular sections of its membership.

Among these groups are now numbered:

The National Contractors Group, consisting of approximately 100 of the largest firms.

The System Builders Section, consisting of all those members who operate industrialized building systems.

The Smaller Firms Committee.

The Painters Committee.

The Plumbers Committee.

The Stonemasons Committee.

The Joinery Committee.

Ensuring that these groups were serviced according to their needs has involved a two-fold exercise by the Federation. On the one hand it has meant establishing a close relationship with the research and other organizations which have sprung up in the industry; on the other the necessity for extending internal Federation facilities to members. Part of this development is to be seen in the work of the active Research and Technical Information Committee, and the appointment of a Technical Advisor whose function is to provide a full advisory and information service to member firms.

Obviously this work necessitates close contact between the NFBTE and the Government's Building Research Station, and with the recently established Construction Industry Research and Information Association. Also important in helping to create greater efficiency in the industry—and better understanding between those initially responsible for its products—is the close contact established with the professions through joint bodies such as the National Joint Consultative Committee of Architects, Quantity Surveyors and Builders.

Increasing government intervention in the industry over the last 20 years has, in addition, led to the creation of organizations such as the Industrial Training Board, and the Economic Development Committee for the Industry, on which the NFBTE has representation and plays a full part in the research and information work which is entailed. It is understandable that, on the NFBTE head office staff, there is a highly qualified economist and statistician. In addition to other duties this official is also responsible for preparing and analysing questionnaires to a cross-section of membership, aimed at collecting information on general trends within the industry.

As the Federation extends its work within this sphere it obviously accumulates experience and information of great value: hence the affiliation of many overseas countries primarily for exchange of information. This kind of "information membership" is also open to individuals, firms and bodies within this country who are not within the building employer category defined by the NFBTE. In practice this class of membership largely consists of materials manufacturers and suppliers, together with a number of local authorities, public authorities and nationalized industries.

The political and industrial pressures which led to these developments of the NFBTE's organization have also raised questions about whether the Federation's basic structure is fitted for the demands now being made upon it. The growing belief that a reappraisal was necessary resulted in the appointment, in 1964, of a working party to consider what changes might be required to meet modern commitments. The working party made a number of suggestions based upon the primary objective that there should be a more closely unified structure, with membership being direct and paying a uniform rate of subscription. Such structural reforms would enable the National Federation to ensure that organization, as a whole, was equally effective throughout the country.

Greater control over total Federation income would also afford the opportunity of being able to subsidize regions which, for various reasons, were not as strong financially as others. In time one of the consequences would be gradual replacement of part-time local association secretaries by full-time officials servicing a group of local associations. Though the Council of the NFBTE accepted the working party's recommendation it will still take time—as it always does in a democratically controlled organization—to bring about a climate of opinion in which changes can be fully implemented.

This is not to imply that matters, at present, stand still in relation to structural improvement. Progress has been made, particularly in replacing part-time personnel by officials devoting their whole energies to the affairs of local associations. It is estimated that, in fact, more than half of the country is now covered by this more effective form of organization. This is, to some extent, a self-generating process. For those employers actively engaged in the work of the NFBTE tend to meet frequently and, as the system of full-time staffing makes its greater effectiveness self-evident, the news of this will spread and accelerate the development in other areas and throughout the Federation generally.

The Main Task

All the diverse activities in which the Federation is engaged do not blur the fact that, in the end, its success or failure depends upon the way in which it handles labour relations. And though there have been two national strikes during the history of the industry, and continuing sporadic disputes, this does not detract from the fact that the NFBTE has approached relationships with the unions in a responsible and reasonable manner. Of course the two sides have had frequent and sometimes lengthy disagreements, but there does not appear to have been the extreme bitterness which has characterized industrial relations in some other industries. This might be due to the fact that the majority of employers were once operatives, or are the sons of one-time operatives.

In addition to this influence there is the fact that the NFBTE always has a number of leading members with long experience of labour negotiations and full-time national officials who, throughout the years, have earned the respect rather than the enmity of the union leaders. Points of view have frequently conflicted, of course, but this has not undermined the mutual sense of confidence and trust without which negotiations are certain to be abortive.

A contributory factor to good relations is the NFBTE's insistence that membership involves responsibility for upholding national agreements entered into with the unions (which may explain why a number of "rogue employers" are reluctant to join). Rule 61 of the NFBTE's Constitution and Rules states firmly that: "Members shall abide by and comply with the provisions of the agreements which at the date of the coming into operation of these Rules subsist between the Federation and the national organizations of Operatives."

Rule 62 goes even further in specifying the penalty for members who do not observe agreed conditions. It affirms that: "Any failure on the part of any Member or body of Members of or affiliated to the Federation to do his or their part in implementing the said agreements involves the Federation in a breach thereof and in the discretion of the Council may entail forfeiture of any claim he or they may have to the support of the Federation."

Of course, the NFBTE no more than any other organization is able to obtain complete observance of its Rules and, in actual practice, there may have been breaches of this undertaking given by employers. In general, however, the NFBTE has shown itself to be a responsible organization which has made an all-round contribution to the improvement and development of the construction industry.

CHAPTER 7

National Joint Council for the Building Industry

A Highly Centralized Machine

Negotiations in the building industry are today highly centralized through one of the most effective national joint councils in British industry. That this is so is a tribute to those leaders of employer and union organizations whose efforts have resulted in a remarkable degree of rationalization being applied in a very complex industry. There are critics who point out that the industry does not present a picture of complete efficiency. They rightly example the conflicting national agreements within the industry and insist that there are too many employer and union organizations. They also add that, for an industry whose products are usually the result of planning, it has not always meticulously planned the development of its own industrial relations machinery.

There is, however, a vast difference between drafting plans for an inanimate structure and the creation of sound, administrative organizations whose development has been subject to the will and moods of the people who brought them into being—and also to the economic and political environment in which they were born. It is certainly true that men on both sides of the industry have generally based their decisions on experience rather than on theoretical plans. But it can justifiably be asserted that these decisions have usually been sound ones which have stood the test of practice. Nor have the builders ever been reluctant to experiment with different forms of negotiating machinery in an attempt to find the one best suited to the changing structure of their industry. In fact the present National Joint Council for the Building Industry

(NJCBI) is basically the end product of such a series of experiments which took place over a period of about 30 years round the turn of this century.

These "experiments" were based on the fact that local and area organizations of joint consultative machinery already existed on quite a widespread basis, and the employers had also created an effective national federation while the unions were slowly struggling towards a similar objective. The one major defect in the industry was that no joint committee yet existed on a national basis for negotiation or conciliation. Among union leaders there was, in fact, violent argument about whether conciliation or arbitration machinery was desirable. There were those who proclaimed that such a course was a betrayal of the long-standing objective that the unions should take over control of the industry. To set-up formal national joint councils seemed to them tantamount to the acceptance of the permanence of the private employers' role and status.

It was, however, internecine union disputes which ultimately gave impetus to new moves for national conciliation machinery. When George Clarke, the General Secretary of the Manchester Unity of Bricklayers, attacked "men", in 1899, "whose lust of conquest and greed of power has very nearly begun to stink in the nostrils of the men in the building trade" he was not slating the employers but indicting the Plasterers Union over a demarcation dispute then taking place between them.[1] This was only one of the demarcation battles then being fought between unions which forced some of their executive committees to accept the conclusion that a form of national conciliation was the only way in which these quarrels could be stopped or ameliorated—even if this meant having to come to terms with the employers.

Proposals were therefore made for the formation of a conciliation board which would "adjust by conciliatory means all questions relating to hours of labour, rates of wages and working rules generally". Though it appeared almost certain that agreement would be reached between both parties these proposals were

[1] *Manchester Unity Quarterly Report*, 30 December 1899.

finally undone because, at the last moment, the employers decided: "It is not expedient to proceed with the formation of a National Board of Conciliation at present unless a monetary guarantee be given on both sides for the carrying out of the decision of the Conciliation Board." The unions were exceedingly suspicious that this pre-supposed "fines" being levied on anyone breaking a decision of the proposed board and they therefore refused to proceed on the basis suggested by the employers. Nevertheless, the plasterers progressed towards an individual agreement with their own employers which had the effect or setting up local conciliation committees to settle grievances which might arise. A central committee was also established to which disputes unresolved at local level could be referred.

Although the majority of unions had rejected the earlier proposals for a national board of conciliation, a continuation of demarcation quarrels and crippling disputes again forced some of them to make another attempt at reaching agreement with employers. As a result:

> A "closer union conference" was held in 1904 between the Yorkshire Master Builders' Association and the various unions of joiners, bricklayers, and masons, to consider the election of local joint councils. The success attending this venture . . . led to the drafting of a larger plan at the end of the year for district conciliation boards, in which the plasterers and plumbers were included, to cover the whole of England.[2]

This was the beginning of the move towards even more effective conciliation machinery, for the success of the experiment begun in Yorkshire led to the creation of the National Board of Conciliation in 1908. This Board was given greater powers and covered almost the whole field of construction activity. There were those, of course, who expected the new Board to achieve miracles and this inevitably led to disappointment in the hearts of the men who thought that it would ultimately achieve complete peace and harmony between employers and operatives. Yet for a relatively short-lived organization, in which the administrative structure was far from perfect, it achieved a great deal. But it could not

[2] R. Postgate, *The Builders' History*, p. 380.

stamp out all disputes in the industry and most certainly did not provide the forum which some wanted for discussing future trends within the industry, nor the unions' pet theme of where ownership should lie. These frustrations led to proposals for amendment of the Board's structure.

With the beginning of the Great War in 1914, however, it seemed as if any further physical development of the joint machinery would have to be postponed though various theories were enthusiastically canvassed on the kind of development which should take place within the industry after the war. One man in particular had a visionary conception for the industry. It was that a Builders' Parliament should be created in which masters and men would meet together in an atmosphere of amity and discuss every issue arising within the industry. The man was Malcolm Sparkes, an employer, who put his theme down on paper and managed to persuade the unions to look at it. The sacrifice demanded from all during the war, he reasoned, would make men more tolerant of new ideas and it should be possible to bring about a congenial atmosphere out of which could be created a harmonious industry from which each man would receive his just reward.

Building Trades Parliament

The Building Trades Parliament (as it was first named) idea was received favourably by most of the union leaders and also met with the approval of the National Federation of Building Trades Employers. Discussion about its structure took place over a period of almost 2 years and, by the time of its first formal meeting in 1918, this had been reasonably defined with the official name changed to the Industrial Council for the Building Industry. In addition to the employer and union organizations the Council also had the support of the then Minister for Reconstruction, the Minister of Labour and the President of the Local Government Board. Its first meetings were held in an atmosphere of mutual goodwill (perhaps with some visions being too roseate) and it had the major objective of finding an answer to the nation's urgent post-war building needs. The Industrial Council did not, however, replace the National Board of Conciliation which continued to function with its terms of reference confined to negotiations on wages and conditions.

Though these matters might appear prosaic compared to the discussions taking place on the Industrial Council they were still the more immediate and realistic issues confronting the industry and of greatest importance to the ordinary workman. The Industrial Council, on the other hand, soared to heights of idealism which were rather naive under the circumstances. Certainly the Council members—all 132 of them—did give time to general debates on the need for greater regularization of wages and measures for the prevention of unemployment. They also went on to theorizing about technical training, research, and better publicity for the industry. Even at this level the Council members were rather moving ahead of themselves and the industry (about 40 years ahead in fact) but it was when they progressed towards a discussion in 1919, on a memorandum presented by a master painter named Thomas Foster, that they lost touch with reality. Foster's scheme envisaged the end of all "speculative" profit and the welding together of the industry as a co-operative whole instead of a competitive complex. The employers' profit would be fixed and he would, in effect, ultimately become an executive.

Foster's scheme in itself was not unsound but it was unreasonably idealistic to believe that the employers were ready for what amounted to industrial suicide or that the unions were yet capable of carrying out their part in such a scheme. Nevertheless it was discussed by the Industrial Council and ultimately adopted. This very fact reveals not that the employers had suddenly become converted to a system of social ownership, but they were already of the belief that the Council was not really capable of making decisions effective. In fact, though the Council lingered on until 1924 before being wound up, it never looked like having great influence on the course of events within the industry.

Meanwhile more realistic work had been done to bring about

improvements in the joint negotiating machinery which led to the formation, in 1921, of the National Wages and Conditions Council for the Building Industry. Under this Council, for the very first time, wages were decided on a national basis. Operatives received an hourly rate which was graded according to the area in which they worked. Altogether there were seventeen different grades brought into existence with differences of a farthing or a halfpenny between each of them.

In addition to this there was an innovation new to industry as a whole and designed to help eliminate disputes over wages: this was the automatic adjustment of wages by linking the standard rate to rises or falls in the Index of Retail Prices (commonly known as the Cost of Living Index). This became known as the Sliding Scale Agreement and, though a number of other industries adopted similar schemes, workers in the construction industry always formed the majority of the total labour force covered by Sliding Scale Agreements.

With the introduction of the National Wages and Conditions Council the basic foundations of the present joint machinery were at last definitely laid. The present National Joint Council for the Building Industry (NJCBI) was, in fact, formed only 5 years after the inauguration of the National Wages and Conditions Council and took over responsibility from it in 1926. Apart from the change of name the most significant alteration was the greater powers given to regional joint wages councils to resolve matters which were capable of being settled at that level.

Since 1926 the NJCBI has endured with its basic procedures being partially amended by occasional changes in its rules. One of the most significant alterations, which has given us the NJC more or less as it exists today, came into operation in January 1932.[3]

[3] The amendment of the NJCBI's Constitution in 1932 was particularly significant in that it united the conciliation with the negotiating process. When the National Wages and Conditions Council was formed in 1921 it concentrated on the negotiation of wages and conditions while leaving conciliation as the preserve of the older National Board of Conciliation. This remained the position when the NJCBI came into existence in 1926. When its Constitution was amended in 1932, however, it took over conciliation responsibilities and the National Board was brought to an end.

The changes arose as a result of discussions begun in 1930 after formal notification by the union side that it wished to terminate the old agreement. One anomaly which was created at this time was that the Scottish employers withdrew completely from the NJC set-up and, in co-operation with the Scottish Region of the National Federation of Building Trades Operatives, established their own Scottish National Joint Council. It was an anomaly because, though they adopted much the same administrative agreement and generally tended to follow NJCBI negotiated awards in England and Wales,[4] discrepancies did arise and especially when Scotland later agreed a reduction in the basic hourly week which threw both hours and wages out of alignment between the countries.

The situation which then existed created such problems that moves were made to bring Scotland back into the fold and, at the same time, to take the necessary steps to bring about gradual uniformity of hours and wages. In April 1964 these moves finally resulted in the merging of the Scottish Council with the NJCBI so that the Council can now claim to negotiate on behalf of all building workers in Great Britain.

The Constitution, Rules and Regulations of the NJCBI were therefore last basically amended when this merger took place. The amendments were not, however, to the principles of the agreement but to allow for the extra representation which became necessary; the Council's total membership being increased from a limit of forty members to forty-six. As the NJC's structure is the most important part of the industrial relations machinery within the building industry its Constitution, Rules and Regulations are given complete in Appendix 2 of this book and the rest of this chapter will, therefore, concentrate on showing how they actually operate in practice.

[4] In Ireland there is another separate National Joint Council in existence on which the Irish Region of the NFBTO negotiates wages and conditions with the Irish employers.

A Three-part Document

The Constitution, Rules and Regulations of the NJCBI is really a three-part document. The first section is the basic Memorandum of Agreement between the adherent bodies stating the principal objectives for which the Council is established. The second part consists of the Rules governing the main procedures of the Council, and the way in which proposals should be submitted. The concluding section on Regulations deals with the actual presentation of proposals before Council members.

On pp. 200–3 is reproduced as Appendix 2 the basic Memorandum of Agreement wherein brief reference is made to the responsibility of the NJC for wages and conditions and also how the Council should be comprised. The powers of regional and local joint committees are also dealt with, as is the question of tackling disputes "with a view to an amicable settlement of the same without resort to strikes or lock-outs".

Perhaps the main point to note from the Memorandum of Agreement is that there is quite a large number of separate bodies who are signatories to the Agreement and, though the unions may decide on a common line of policy through the National Federation of Building Trades Operatives, they are nevertheless treated as individual adherent bodies of the NJCBI and are entitled to the right of individual decision on any matter before the Council. Their agreement to make common cause through the NFBTO is purely voluntary and does not compromise their rights on the NJC.

In an earlier chapter it was explained that not all the unions affiliated to the NFBTO are represented on the National Joint Council. The following are the unions which are adherent bodies:

Amalgamated Society of Woodworkers,
Amalgamated Society of Painters and Decorators,
Plumbing Trades Union,
Amalgamated Slaters', Tilers' and Roofing Operatives' Society,
National Association of Operative Plasterers,

Amalgamated Union of Building Trade Workers,
Amalgamated Society of Woodcutting Machinists,
Transport and General Workers' Union,
National Union of General and Municipal Workers,
Scottish Plasterers' Union,
Scottish Slaters, Tilers and Roofing Operatives.

In addition the NFBTO is itself an adherent body entitled to send representatives.

The numbers of employers' associations which are adherent bodies of the NJC are much fewer in number because they have reached a greater measure of co-ordination than the unions and therefore only three federations of employers are signatories to the agreement. These are the:

National Federation of Building Trades Employers,
National Federation of Plumbers and Domestic Engineers,
National Federation of Roofing Contractors.

The Council of forty-six members is divided equally between employer and union organizations and in the Rules of the NJC (reproduced on pp. 204–17) are laid down the essentials of the detailed machinery by which the principles of the Memorandum of Agreement are to be effected. It is in this section too that emphasis is laid on each side of the NJC being treated as a separate entity for the purpose of decision-making. Any proposal before the Council can only be agreed if the employers carry it by a majority among themselves and likewise the operatives' organizations. There can be no cross-voting so no possibility arises of decisions being made by a combined majority of employer and operatives voting together. (This was a situation which existed on the old National Wages and Conditions Council and at least one important decision was made by cross-voting.)

The NJC has three regular meetings each year in February, July and October, though other meetings may be called if necessary—such as when a major wage negotiation is taking place. The February meeting of the Council is regarded as the annual meeting at which the accounts are examined and the officers of the Council elected. These consist of a Chairman and Vice-Chairman and are elected from among the members of the Council. Traditionally the Chairman comes from the employers' side and the Vice-Chairman from the operatives. In addition to these honorary officials there are also two Honorary Joint Secretaries of the Council, one appointed by each side. The secretary of the employers' side is usually a senior official of the NFBTE, while the secretary of the operatives' side is the secretary of the NFBTO. Of course, it is obvious that these honorary secretaries, who have great responsibilities within their own federations, could not administer the extensive organization of the NJC. A permanent official, the Clerk to the Council, is therefore appointed to take over control as an impartial administrative officer.

That the NJC is very much more than a body confining itself to regulating basic wages and conditions can be seen from the number of committees that are appointed by the Council to cover various aspects of its work. Rule 2 (b) in Appendix 2 gives the titles of these committees and shows that they cover almost every aspect of the industry's operations including apprenticeship training, safety, health and welfare. The National Joint Apprenticeship Board is itself a remarkable example of the beneficial work carried out by the Council. Though unfortunately not every apprentice is yet covered by a formal deed of indenture, the Apprenticeship Board is symbolic of a registration system which now covers the majority of youths entering the crafts and involves employers and operatives, from national right down to local level, in safeguarding the interests of apprentices.

Of course the main duty of the NJC is to decide the wages and conditions which will apply in the industry and clause 5 of the Memorandum of Agreement in Appendix 2 shows these cover a very wide field. All the decisions taken on these matters are contained in what most employer and union officials regard as the "bible" of the industry—the National Working Rules (which are dealt with in the later chapter on wages and conditions). For a supposedly very backward industry the leading men on the NJC have also shown that they are not reluctant to go beyond the formal rules where they thought it necessary to meet the challenge of the times.

One classic example of this spirit took place in 1962 just after the Government established the National Economic Development Council (NEDC). Although it was not then generally recognized that for the NEDC to achieve its maximum potential it would need to be linked to appropriate committees for each major industry, the building industry leaders were sufficiently alive to the situation to form their own Economic Planning Advisory Council for the Construction Industries. Its terms of reference were: "to consult together on matters affecting the Construction Industries relating to general economic development, and to advise the Government as appropriate". Here the employer and union leaders had willingly stepped outside the confines of the NJCBI because they felt it necessary in view of current economic development. The Planning Council they established was so successful in its voluntary efforts that it was with reluctance that it was allowed to go out of existence when the economic development committees for building and civil engineering were created.

Democratic Organization at All Levels

Apart from showing this kind of pragmatic approach the NJC has always prided itself on being a democratic organization allowing opportunities for full participation by the employers and operatives at all levels, for its rules provide for the delegation of certain powers to regional, area and local joint committees. Of these the most important are the regional committees on which sit thirty members, comprising fifteen from employers and fifteen from union organizations. The areas of jurisdiction of the ten regional joint councils of the NJC and the addresses of the honorary joint secretaries are given in Appendix 3. It is these councils which may initiate amendments to vary the National Working Rules to suit the particular circumstances of the regions for which they are responsible. They also have the task of adjudicating on disputes arising within their regions. For this purpose they must establish standing regional conciliation panels which, in effect, act as "courts of first hearing".

The regional council also has the right to determine whether or not area joint committees should be appointed and, if it decides to set one up, has the power to define its composition and functions. In addition the regional council maintains close association with local joint committees. Even at this local level considerable responsibility rests with the employer and operative members of the committee. The regularization of overtime working, fixing of the "free area" boundaries and general control of the operation of the Working Rules in their localities come within their jurisdiction. Also, although the local committees are not recognized under the national rules as having the right to first hearings in matters of dispute, they sometimes exercise this function.

This, then, is a brief outline of the formal machinery of the NJCBI (which is shown in diagrammatic form in Fig. 5) and an indication of the duties which each level of the organization assumes. But how does the negotiation and conciliation machinery actually work in practice? If we consider first the machinery for settling disputes the quality of participation is fully revealed, as is the fact that the industry is justified in having pride in its achievements in this direction. There are two major methods of settling disputes within the building industry. One is through the official conciliation procedure of the NJC and is specifically intended for issues falling within the Council's jurisdiction; that is in disputes which arise over the agreements embodied within the National Working Rules.

The second method is that arising under the Emergency Disputes Agreement and is for settling those grievances not falling within the scope of the NJC conciliation machinery. Disputes which would come within this category might be over demarcation or alleged victimization of union stewards.

Obviously most problems will be resolved through the NJC's official conciliation procedure. This is brought into action when any matter which is incapable of settlement between employer

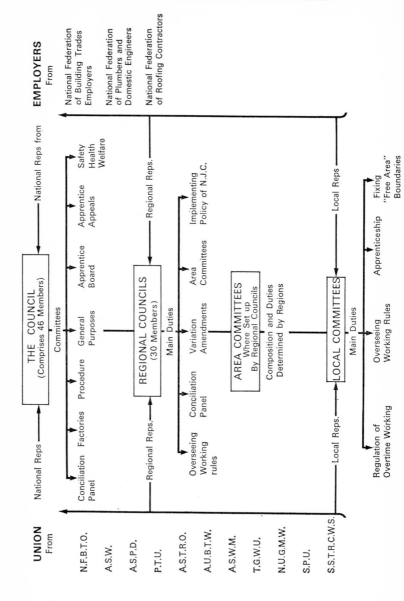

and operative at site level is referred to the regional conciliation panel. (As already explained, the local joint committee might undertake this initial conciliation even though they do not have the formal powers of a court of first hearing. They have been successful in bringing about amicable settlements in a number of cases without the matter going any further.) As undue delay in hearing cases and making decisions would obviously bring the machinery into disrepute—and lead increasingly to disputes being fought out on sites—the Rules state that all cases referred to the regional conciliation panel should be heard as soon as possible and within 21 days at most.

The regional panel is comprised equally of employers and operatives' representatives none of whom are directly involved in the dispute. When the panel meets the employers and operatives concerned in the dispute (or their representatives), together with witnesses, are allowed to give evidence before the panel members who then make a decision on the issue. Any decision they make is binding upon the parties concerned—subject to their right to appeal against it within 7 days to the Clerk to the National Joint Council.

If an appeal is made this is tantamount to asking for a rehearing of the case before the national conciliation panel, with the whole matter again being thrashed out in an attempt to bring about a decision. Usually most disputes are successfully terminated at this level and no further action is required. Of course the point arises that, if a matter can be referred upwards because it was not possible to reach an amicable joint decision at regional level, this can happen at national level also. This fact is recognized and the conciliation machinery provides for such possibility. In the event of disagreement on the national conciliation panel the matter goes a stage further in that it is reported to the next meeting of the full National Joint Council together with all relevant minutes and documents of the case.

The Council's responsibility is to probe for a solution which it can refer back for consideration by the national conciliation panel or, alternatively, it could remit the matter to a special committee under the terms of Rule 13, in Appendix 2. If the dispute ultimately proved so obdurate that it could not be settled within the industry's machinery the final step would be for the NJC to arrange for outside arbitration.

It can be clearly seen, from this detailed procedure, that even though building is a highly fragmented industry the conciliation process of the NJC is designed to ensure a thorough investigation of any grievance which may arise. Each operative in the industry knows that should he have a dispute with his employer on-site, even a small site in some obscure part of the country, his appeal for justice may proceed from local to national level with perhaps even outside arbitration in an attempt to give him a fair hearing.

Green Book Procedure

The other method of resolving disputes which has been referred to is that which takes place under the National Emergency Disputes Agreement. This procedure, in effect, complements the conciliation machinery of the NJC. The National Emergency Disputes Agreement arose from the fact that, very soon after the formation of the NJC in 1926, it was realized that some of the disputes within the industry would not turn on an interpretation of the National Working Rules. Even in cases where they did it could not always be assumed that the operative or operatives concerned would be willing to remain at work while awaiting the adjudication of conciliation panels on their grievances. A more spontaneous reaction might be to come out on strike.

It was to cover these various possibilities that the Emergency Disputes Agreement was made on 8 July 1927 (as it was a separate agreement and issued as a pamphlet with green covers it has become generally known in the industry as the "Green Book Procedure"). This agreement is contained in full in Appendix 4 of this book. The significant point to note is that it is not an NJC agreement between all its adherent organizations but a separate one made by the two major national bodies in the industry; the NFBTE and NFBTO. Responsibility for operating this emergency procedure therefore lies upon them and not the National Joint

Council. Also the findings reached by any dispute commission set up under the agreement are enforceable only through the national executives of the employers' and operatives' federations. The major objectives of the emergency procedure can be stated quite briefly; to avoid strikes by speedily resolving grievances which might arise on-site and, which if undue delay occurred, could lead to a stoppage of work.

Where such a possibility arises the first step is that all the relevant details have to be forwarded as soon as possible to the local officials of the employers' and operatives' organizations. As detailed in the Regulations, Part One of Appendix 4, an obligation then rests on these officials to keep their headquarters informed about events and, pending formal adjudication on the issue, to take all necessary action to prevent any stoppage of work. The effect of the Emergency Disputes Procedure being brought into play is that, at all levels, officers of both federations are engaged in trying to seek a peaceful solution to the dispute. Initially advice and encouragement will be aimed at reaching a speedy settlement at site level. If this proves impossible to bring about then an official Emergency Disputes Commission is convened either at regional or national level according to the circumstances. In each case the commission is composed of three employers' and three operatives' representatives who are appointed *ad hoc* as the need arises. In addition they are attended by one official from each of their respective federations. The personnel for the commission will be drawn from the regional councils of the employers' and operatives' federations if it is held at this level. Where the need for a national commission arises the members are generally drawn from the national executives of the NFBTE and NFBTO.

The first duty of the commission is to take evidence from all the parties involved in the dispute. When they have done this they may decide that the issue is one that should more appropriately be settled through the normal conciliation machinery of the NJCBI and they will accordingly direct that it be so referred. But in those cases where the dispute does not come under the National Working Rules, or other matters relevant to the National Joint

Council, then it is up to the commission itself to consider the matter and make recommendations to the national executive committees of the employers' and operatives' federations for settlement of the dispute.

It is in this latter eventuality that full responsibility of ensuring compliance with the commission's recommendations rests squarely upon the national executives of both federations. In any one year there is an average of about fourteen or fifteen cases which are dealt with by national emergency disputes commissions and almost without exception decisions reached by them are implemented by the two sides. Should there be any further difficulty, however, the procedure provides that a special joint conference of the executive members of both federations should take place in order to try and reach a decision.

In general the joint machinery has worked well. Of course there are criticisms that at times it works too slowly. But when one considers that the machinery attempts to adjudicate on disputes with the same fairness and thoroughness of a law court (and when one considers the time which can be taken to reach decisions in the law courts!) it can be claimed that it has reasonably fulfilled its purpose of keeping down the number of stoppages that take place within the industry. In fact, the employers have in the past frequently made favourable comments about the "harmonious relationships" within the construction industry compared with others. Of late, however, they have tended to be more critical. In their statement of evidence to the Royal Commission on Trades Unions and Employers Associations (paragraphs 68 and 69) the NFBTE states that: "Official strikes are uncommon in building. Unofficial disputes are common on the larger jobs and in areas of intense building activity." The statement goes on to claim that this is often due to the contempt shown by some local officials and stewards for the official machinery. It further adds that the situation also arises because "the central authority of trade union executives has weakened and there is less respect shown for negotiated agreements". The employers conclude by deducing from all this that there should be legal action taken to curb the "impunity" with which workers in construction come out on strike.

From this one would suppose that the situation in construction had become rather serious in recent years. Certainly when given the facts that construction is a highly complex industry, with a largely casual labour force and a sporadic system of operations, an objective observer would probably anticipate that days lost through strikes in the industry would be generally higher than in others. Accepting that one or two areas of "intense building activity" do tend to have a higher degree of unofficial action the fact is, nevertheless, that construction compares very favourably with other industries as far as strikes are concerned. Table 9 shows this quite clearly. It gives the figures for total days lost in each year through disputes in all industries, then the number of days lost in construction and their percentage of the total. The key to interpreting the figures given in the table is that the labour force in construction has formed about 7 per cent of the total number of employees in employment in Great Britain during this period (at the moment construction has approximately 1,750,000 out of a total of 24,550,000 employees at work in the country).[5]

Table 9 shows that in each year the average of working days lost in construction is normally below its percentage share of the total labour force. The year 1963, of course, shows a steep rise in days lost but this was due to the fact that this was an exceptional year in which a national strike occurred over a wages dispute.

And even though this brief summary of the position indicates that construction has a reasonably good record, a really clear picture cannot be obtained unless one realizes that the overall total of employees against which construction is being compared includes sections in which professional, clerical, and administrative staffs predominate and for whom strike action is a comparatively rare event. To obtain a more equitable comparison we must

[5] Again it must be pointed out that while this chapter relates specifically to private construction on the building side, it is not possible to obtain statistics which give separate figures for building as against civil engineering and the figures in Table 9 are for the total labour force employed in the industry.

contrast construction with similar heavy industries. It is when we do this that we see construction emerging with a very good record as far as disputes are concerned.

Take for comparison the Ministry of Labour classification "Metals, engineering, shipbuilding and vehicles". Over the same 10-year period shown in Table 9 this group, which comprises about

TABLE 9. WORKING DAYS LOST THROUGH INDUSTRIAL DISPUTES, 1956–65

Year	In thousands		Construction as percentage of total
	All industries and services	Construction	
1956	2083	78	3·75
1957	8412	84	0·99
1958	3462	151	4·46
1959	5270	138	2·62
1960	3024	110	3·64
1961	3046	285	9·35
1962	5798	222	3·85
1963	1755	356	20·29
1964	2277	125	5·49
1965	2993	134	4·57
Totals	38,060	1683	Average 4·42

20 per cent of the total number of employees at work in the country, was responsible for approximately 54 per cent of all working days lost through disputes.

This classification, with engineering as its broad basis, has not been taken because it provides the worst example against which construction will obviously shine. Arthur Marsh has pointed out that it is generally topped by other industries and that "since the war, engineering has usually taken at least fourth place in working days lost per thousand employees behind coal mining, shipbuilding and port and inland transport".[6] Construction has therefore a

⁶ A. Marsh, *Industrial Relations in Engineering*, p. 134.

good record in this matter and, in view of the nature of the industry and the fact that undoubted "trouble spots" exist, the men responsible for setting up the joint machinery and maintaining it in action can claim that it has stood the test of time.

A Quasi-judicial Atmosphere

Perhaps one of the major contributory factors of that success is the quasi-judicial atmosphere in which the major NJC committees tend to work. Normally when one considers negotiations between employers and unions the concept is of confrontation between the two sides, with direct argument and exchange taking place between the leading protagonists. The Regulations of the NJC, however (which form the third section of the document setting out the Constitution, Rules and Regulations), avoid this kind of confrontation. Instead the Regulations speak in legal terminology about "Evidence and Witnesses" and that "only direct evidence" can be admitted during discussions. The spirit of these Regulations is also carried out in actual practice and this is perhaps revealed most clearly when major negotiations on wages and conditions are taking place on the National Joint Council itself. In fact the atmosphere at this level is usually in sharp contrast to the rhetoric and passion generated when claims are being formulated. We can see this clearly if we follow the line of action through from the initial to the final stages.

In the main the first move towards negotiations comes from the trade-union side for, although the NJC provides that employers' organizations have the same opportunity for making proposals, it is generally the union side in industry which takes the initiative by proposing amendments for improving wages and conditions. Therefore the first signs of action are seen among the thousands of local branches of the unions affiliated to the NFBTO. At this level ideas are put forward which result in motions being submitted for consideration at the various union annual conferences. Debate by the delegates will lead to the adoption of certain of the motions as union policy. After this they are usually refined by the national executives concerned and then forwarded for discussion to the Central Council of the NFBTO. And, in the same way that compromise at union conferences results in commonly accepted policy within a particular union, so the same process takes place on the Central Council of the NFBTO leading ultimately to a Federation policy on wages and conditions to be presented to the employers through the National Joint Council for the Building Industry.

At each level of the internal union debate the various proposals may be thrashed out amid passion, prejudice and fervent argument, but when the final stage of presenting the claim through the NJC arrives the mood abruptly changes as the formal procedure takes over. Each separate proposal amending the Constitution of the NJC has to be notified to the Clerk to the Council 8 weeks prior to the date of the meeting at which the proposal is to be discussed. (Until a few years ago these major constitutional amendments on wages and conditions could only be put forward at the annual meeting of the NJC but the Rules were changed to allow for presentation of such matters to any of the three regular meetings which take place each year.)

When the Clerk receives such proposals from the NFBTO or an adherent union, or perhaps from an employers' organization, he must circulate them to all the other adherent parties to the NJC who are then allowed 14 days within which to send constitutional amendment notices themselves.[7]

Though it is Rule 10 of the NJC which outlines this procedure for submission—and the ultimate ratification—of such constitutional amendments, it is to the Regulations, clauses 1–7, we must turn to find the unique manner in which they are actually presented and discussed. Clause 1 lays down that proposals "shall

---

[7] As shown by the NJC Rules, in Appendix 2, the Council actually deals with two kinds of amendments: the Constitutional and the Variation amendments. It is the Constitutional amendment which is the major one while the Variation amendment, as explained in the Rules, is to meet requests originating within the Regions.

be definitely and specifically drawn up by the Secretary of the Party concerned". This is so that Council members may be able to read the proposal in full and, therefore, be able to give a considered decision on the matter. In practice this means that the party submitting an amendment must prepare a statement of case and a copy of this is given to every Council member. Where this statement of case concerns a claim from the union side for increased wages or betterment of conditions the employers might put in a counter-amendment based on a document which, in effect, is a rebuttal of the union's case.

When the actual Council meeting takes place at which the constitutional amendments are to be discussed there is no question of the antagonists facing each other across a long table. There is no table in fact; all the members of the Council sit facing a raised platform on which are the Chairman, Vice-Chairman, Honorary Joint Secretaries, Clerk to the Council and other officials. By tradition the trade-union representatives sit in a solid block on the Chairman's right and the employers to his left. Between both sides and directly in front of the Chairman is a row of seats which are not occupied by members of the Council. These are for the representatives and the witnesses who will be presenting the proposals for the adherent parties which have submitted them.

When the Chairman announces the hearing of a particular proposal, say, for a major wage claim the representative putting the case for the NFBTO is brought into the Council chamber and is normally accompanied by the research officer of the Federation who may sit beside him during the time the case is being put and give any advice which might be necessary. In front of them will be the employers' representative who will be putting the NFBTE document opposing the case, and he is usually accompanied by an expert from the staff of that Federation. At the invitation of the Chairman the NFBTO representative rises and puts his claim. He may do this by simply reading out the written statement of case already in the hands of NJC members or by making a short speech in support of it. The same right to make a statement is also accorded to the employers' representative.

After the statements have been made comes the "cross-examination" to which all witnesses are subject according to regulations. By custom the representatives who put the opposing cases are first allowed to cross-examine each other attempting, in doing so, to bring out points calculated to undermine each other's argument. After this the members of the NJC, under the Chairman's jurisdiction, are allowed to put questions in much the same way as questions might be put to witnesses in a court of law. The trade-union side will obviously put what can be termed "leading questions" to the union spokesman, thus giving him an opportunity to enlarge on the reasons why his proposal should be endorsed by the Council. Conversely employer members will ask hostile questions designed to embarrass the union case. When it is the turn of the employers' representatives to come under fire the attitude of the Council members is, of course, reversed! In such a situation it is obvious that there is not scope for passionate debate. There cannot exist such a possibility when the opposing sides of the Council are prohibited from directly addressing each other; their remarks must always be phrased in the form of questions to the representatives who put the cases forward. And these representatives, in turn, act very much like "witnesses in the box" giving their replies in as objective a manner as possible.

When all the cross-examination has been concluded the Council could, of course, proceed to make a decision. It would be expecting too much, however, for an immediate decision on really vital issues concerning basic wage rates and working conditions. The usual procedure has therefore been for the Council to refer proposals to committee with instructions that they report back after further examination of the matters concerned. Though this stage may often take up some months of time it is usually the method by which agreement is finally obtained, and all that remains is for the Council to endorse any recommendations from the committee and then submit them to the adherent parties for formal ratification.

There have, of course, been occasions during the post-war period when the industry's internal procedure has been gone through to the final stages and an issue still remained unresolved. In circumstances like this Rule 13(b) provides that where deadlock arises the matter should be referred to outside arbitration and "The method of arbitration shall be determined in each case by a majority of the Council present and voting". Arbitration decisions have usually concluded negotiations because the awards are accepted, however reluctantly, by both sides.

The one notable exception to this occurred in 1963 when the difficult wage negotiations then taking place in the industry were ultimately referred to the then recently established National Incomes Commission. The unions were extremely incensed about this because they refused to accept that the Commission had any authority to interfere in their negotiations, or to cut across the joint machinery which had been established. The situation then arose that while the employers co-operated with the Commission, attended its hearings and gave evidence, the unions bluntly refused to follow suit. For the first time there was a really significant and serious cleavage between employers and unions about the course of arbitration and the unions ultimately brought their members out on strike. It was the first national dispute confined to the construction industry since the conflict of 1924 and this strike was responsible for the jump in 1963 of the total days lost through disputes as shown in Table 9. Nevertheless, neither the number of operatives involved nor the length of the strike were as serious as the one which occurred in 1924.

On the whole the machinery for governing relations between employers and operatives in the building industry has functioned well. In recent years, however, changes have taken place in other spheres and these have impinged upon the Council's traditional responsibilities (such as the impact of Industrial Training Legislation in relation to the NJC's work and responsibility on apprenticeship). Nevertheless the National Joint Council has usually responded in a reasoned and helpful manner to any such developments. In fact its empirical approach to these problems is typical of the spirit which has animated the Council from the outset and which has been responsible for much of its success.

CHAPTER 8

Civil Engineering

The Scope of Civil Engineering

Though a separate national industrial agreement exists for work done in the civil engineering section of the construction industry there are no reliable figures of the number of men, or the proportion of the total construction programme, which it covers. This is one aspect of the situation arising in the industry due to its division into building and civil engineering sections. Official government statistics about the industry shy away from making estimates of the proportions of work and men involved in each section and the National Economic Development Council, in its early report on Construction, hardly clarifies the situation by simply affirming that: "Construction is a shorthand term covering a wide range of activities in civil engineering and building."

The closest one can get to an authorative statement about civil engineering, by a leading figure in that field, is the estimate made by Mr. W. G. Mitchell, President of the Federation of Civil Engineering Contractors, in 1962 that: "Of Britain's total capital investment about half goes into construction, and some 30 per cent of this is attributable to civil engineering works."[1]

As the present total value of output in construction is well over £4000 million annually this would give civil engineering credit for a proportion amounting to something near £1400 million.[2] If we accept this as being a reasonable estimate of output

[1] From an article by Mr. W. G. Mitchell in the 1962 *Financial Times* Survey on Civil Engineering.

[2] This figure is for output by all sectors, both private and public.

from civil engineering it does not automatically follow that, in proportion, about one-third of the construction industry's labour force is involved in its production. Civil engineering is more capital intensive than most forms of construction work. In fact, at the opposite extreme the repairs and maintenance sector within building is the most labour intensive within construction.

It is, therefore, not possible to accurately assess by reference to volume of output the number of men who are, at any one time, covered by agreements entered into by employers and unions represented on the joint organization for this sector of the industry—the Civil Engineering Construction Conciliation Board for Great Britain (CECCB). This Board is the other major joint industrial body within the construction industry and one which many exclusively building unions assert could link up with the National Joint Council for the Building Industry to make one effective agreement covering the whole of construction.

The existence of the two agreements has, in fact, led to a certain amount of hostility. Symbolic of the atmosphere which has tended to cloud the workings of the CECCB is its own challenging statement in the fourth clause of the Board's constitution:

> that all parties hereto accept the principle that the Civil Engineering industry and the Building Trade are essentially separate and distinct and will negotiate conditions for the Civil Engineering Industry with that fact in view recognising that the Civil Engineering industry as in the past should be subject to its own Working Rule Agreement which should take account of its own peculiar circumstances.[3]

Of course, one of the growing problems is the often recurring difficulty of deciding exactly what is civil engineering as against building work. It is simple enough to state that roads, sewerage, water supply, dams, tunnels, bridges, hydroelectric schemes and the like are civil engineering works. But there is an increasingly large area of operations, especially with the growing use of reinforced concrete for many purposes, where the division is not clear and where genuine resentment takes place over which national agreement should apply to a particular job.

[3] Page 2 of the *Constitution of the Board.*

Due to the resentment which is sometimes roused on the building side there are those who tend to think of the NJCBI as the original joint machinery for the industry and believe the CECCB to be a relatively recent and thrusting upstart in construction. In fact the Board dates back its foundation to December of 1919 and is at least as old as the NJCBI in its present form. The first signatories to the agreement which established the Board in 1919 consisted of the Federation of Civil Engineering Contractors —the only employer body—and the National Amalgamated Union of Enginemen, Firemen, Mechanics, Motormen and Electrical Workers. In addition to this union there were other operatives' organizations representing labourers which, through time, were amalgamated into the two present-day large general workers unions.

In view of the present hostility shown by the majority of building unions to the CECCB it is surprising that it was ever successfully established initially—considering union facts at that time. The traditional unions in the industry, mainly organizing craftsmen, had formed the NFBTO in 1918 and it was accepted as the most powerful operatives' voice in construction. The weight of the Federation was solidly behind the then National Board of Conciliation (NBC) as the official negotiating authority for the industry. And, in fact, what effective agreements there were had evolved through the NBC.

Though the civil engineering section of construction was far enough developed for the employers to have already created their organization, the Federation of Civil Engineering Contractors (FCEC), it existed basically for trading matters and not those concerning industrial agreements. Wages and conditions for men on civil engineering work usually centred around those agreed by the NBC. Where specialized operations were involved any plus-rates given arose from negotiations on-site between the men and the firm concerned. The civil engineering employers were not, however, content with this situation. The working rules evolved through the National Board of Conciliation were obviously based upon traditional building practice and, thought

the FCEC, did not meet the requirements of civil engineering·
For these reasons the FCEC tended to remain aloof from the
machinery of the NBC though it was obvious that, without the
co-operation of at least some of the unions, they would be unable
to proceed very far in forming alternative joint industrial machinery to their own satisfaction.

That they finally received this co-operation was due, in great
part, to internecine squabbling among the building unions.
When the NFBTO had been formed it originally admitted two
labourers' unions into affiliation. But a scattering of other
labourers' organizations still remained outside, basically because
the Federation set down certain prior requirements before it
would consent to allow them in. It insisted that consultations
should take place on amalgamation between the different labourers' unions and that, once inside the NFBTO, there should be no
treading on the craft organizations' toes by the occasional
"poaching" of membership. At first it seemed as if the labourers'
unions concerned would attempt to comply with the conditions
of entry, for amalgamation discussions were entered into by four
of them.

Then the Navvies' Union was pulled out of the talks by their
thrusting General Secretary, "Navvy" Ward, who decided that
eminence for his organization lay in another direction. Control
over the conditions under which his members worked, he thought,
could best be obtained by going direct to the civil engineering
employers and offering to come to agreement with them. Given
his lead some of the other labourers' unions decided to take the
same line of policy. Ward also had the encouragement of Ben
Tillet of the Dock, Wharf and Riverside Workers' Union in his
efforts.

News that "Navvy" Ward had approached the civil engineering
employers to conclude an industrial agreement certainly made
the NFBTO affiliates apprehensive about the outcome. But they
were now frustrated in doing anything about the matter because
of their earlier attitude towards Ward and his colleagues. They
could not be dictated to because they were outwith the Federation

and had nothing to lose by any steps they took. Nor could the federated unions try to warn off the civil engineering employers by taking industrial action: Ward and his colleagues would quite happily supply men to any site threatened with closure over this particular matter.

The theoretically all powerful NFBTO unions had therefore to look on helplessly while Ward and his colleagues concluded discussion with the civil engineering employers finally leading, in 1919, to the introduction of the Civil Engineering Conciliation Board.[4]

Signatories to the Agreement

The signatories to the original agreement were, therefore, the various labourers' unions involved in the discussions led by "Navvy" Ward. Since that time amalgamations, and shifts in policy, have led to a considerable change in the situation and the present signatories to the CECCB Working Rule Agreement are:

> The Federation of Civil Engineering Contractors,
> Transport and General Workers' Union,
> National Union of General and Municipal Workers,
> National Union of Enginemen, Firemen, Mechanics, and Electrical Workers,
> Amalgamated Union of Building Trade Workers,
> Amalgamated Society of Woodworkers,
> National Federation of Building Trades Operatives.

The inclusion of the craft unions as parties to the CECCB is relatively recent and was agreed at a meeting in July 1951. This significant change in the constitution was effected in recognition of the fact that a number of craftsmen were employed on works of a civil engineering nature and therefore they should be allowed

[4] No published material exists which gives a picture of these particular events. I am indebted for the historical outline recounted here to Sir Richard Coppock, ex-General Secretary of the NFBTO, who gave me this account during an interview with him (W.S.H.).

representatives: "who would form an integral part of the Operatives' side of the Board and have a full voice in the determination of wages, hours and working conditions of operatives employed in the Civil Engineering industry."

The presence of craft union representatives does not, of course, alter the fact that the general workers' unions have a predominant voice on the operatives' side of the CECCB. The full Board has at the moment nineteen members with representation consisting of:

(a) An Operatives' Panel not exceeding thirteen in number comprising:
   Four representatives of the Transport and General Workers' Union;
   Four representatives of the National Union of General and Municipal Workers;
   One representative of the National Union of Enginemen, Firemen, Mechanics and Electrical Workers;
   Four representatives of Craftsmen, two of whom shall be representative of Woodworkers and one of Bricklayers, these being the crafts continuously and predominantly employed in the Civil Engineering industry.
(b) An Employers' Panel comprising six representatives nominated by the Federation.

On the operatives' side it can be seen that the general workers unions take nearly 70 per cent of the places available. The fourth class of operative representation, relating particularly to craftsmen, is comprised of two representatives of the Amalgamated Society of Woodworkers, one from the Amalgamated Union of Building Trade Workers and the other place is generally held by the Secretary of the National Federation of Building Trades Operatives. He, in fact, is regarded as a kind of joint representative of all the other craftsmen working within the Civil Engineering section of construction and who are affiliated to his Federation.

The fact that the employers have only six representatives on the Board, from the Federation of Civil Engineering Contractors, does not mean that they can be submerged by the operatives' votes. On the Conciliation Board both sides, for the purpose of decision-making, vote within their own panels. On a proposition before the Board, therefore, the operatives would take a poll among the thirteen members of their panel to see if it could attract a majority; the employers among their six. Only an affirmative vote of the majority within each of the panels can make a proposal effective.

These two panels are particularly significant in the machinery of the CECCB for they are its basic organizational feature. Each panel appoints its own Chairman and Secretary to conduct internal panel business. By contrast the main Board of the CECCB has no regular Chairman defined by rule, nor regular meetings but is to be "held at such times and places as the occasion may require and shall be convened by the Secretaries at the request of either Panel".

One of the Board's major tasks—second to making agreements on wages and conditions for civil engineering—is its role of final conciliator during disputes. The actual machinery of conciliation is, however, relatively simple when compared to that of the National Joint Council for the Building Industry. In the first instance the resolving of a dispute is laid upon the employer or the agent representing him on the site where the dispute has broken out. The rule specifies that either of them:

> shall at the earliest opportunity meet the workman or a deputation of the workmen concerned for the mutual discussion of any question in the settlement of which both parties are directly concerned and failing agreement, if it is agreed by the Employer or his Agent and such accredited full-time official or officials of the operative parties to this Agreement (hereinafter called "Accredited Representatives") as represent the workman or workmen concerned that the question affects only the particular work of construction a further endeavour, if desired, may be made to negotiate a settlement between the Employer or his Agent and the Accredited Representative or Representatives of the workman or workmen concerned.

The basic responsibility therefore for settling disputes lies upon management and the operatives' representatives at site level. However, if no settlement can be reached at this stage, or if the operatives' representatives claim that the matter in dispute "is of a general character affecting the interests of the Employers and Operatives as a body, either party to the dispute shall prior to a stoppage of work refer the matter to the Board for settlement".

The conciliation procedure is therefore very straightforward. The matter is either resolved on-site or referred direct to the Board of the CECCB for settlement. Although it might be thought that this rule leaves it open for the Board to be swamped with appeals for conciliation it should be remembered that civil engineering jobs are usually much larger than building projects and are not nearly so numerous. The CECCB has, therefore, usually found itself capable of dealing with the unresolved-at-site level grievances referred to it.

The Working Rule Agreement

The basic wage rates and conditions laid down in the Working Rule Agreement of the CECCB do not radically differ from those in the building industry. This is to be expected because general working conditions for operatives do not greatly differ whether engaged on building or civil engineering projects. There are certain areas within each field, of course, where this is not true but construction operatives generally face the problems and hazards of casual labour, inclement weather, safety, health and welfare risks whether on building or civil engineering sites.[5]

One of the most important distinctions is that the CECCB Working Rule Agreement gives pride of place to the establishment of a large range of plus-rates for workmen in the industry and, to a great extent, the fixing of these rates is the main reason for the Board's existence. Another basic difference between the working rule agreements is that the civil engineering rules do not provide for the tight control over overtime which is a feature of the rules for the building industry. In the civil engineering working rules there are also special provisions for work such

[5] Because of the basic similarity on wages and other matters, Chapter 9 on wages and conditions will be used to outline conditions applying to construction workers generally except where civil engineering's special rules are noted in this chapter.

as tunnelling, tidal, roads and other operations particular to that section of the construction industry.

On the question of wage rates the Rules for civil engineering make a significant terminological distinction from the building industry agreement. They do not refer to labourers' rates of pay and, in fact, affirm to the contrary "that the problem of labourers attendant upon craftsmen will cease to exist since all labourers employed in the industry shall be regarded as Civil Engineering labourers whether attendant upon a craftsman or not". From this line of reasoning the agreement then proceeds to further eliminate the word "labourer" so that basic wage rates are referred to in relation to "general civil engineering operatives".

Apart from this differing emphasis on terminology, however, the basic wage rates of the CECCB are on similar lines to those agreed for building. There is the same special rate for craftsmen and general civil engineering operatives employed in London and Liverpool, and the Class 1 rate (which is equivalent to Grade "A" building rates for craftsmen and labourers) for the rest of the country. The bringing into line of civil engineering rates with building, however, dates back as recently as 1951 at the time when the Constitution of the CECCB was altered to allow for craft representation. Previous to this the CECCB had recognized only a fixed rate for general civil engineering workers, upon which all plus-rates were based. Even the wages paid to craftsmen were grossed up on this civil engineering rate plus varied amounts according to skill.

Earnings Compared with Building

It is often assumed that because civil engineering operations involve more labourers compared with the craft intensive building side that earnings will be lower than in building. This is not, however, the case. Though separate statistics are no longer published for building as against civil engineering earnings, they were collected by the Ministry concerned up to 1959. These figures showed that civil engineering earnings (basic rates together with plus-rates, overtime and bonus) were drawing very much ahead of those in the building industry. Table 10 gives four particular years from which the trend can be clearly seen.

TABLE 10. AVERAGE WEEKLY EARNINGS IN BUILDING
AND CIVIL ENGINEERING[6]

Year	Building	Civil engineering	Percentage by which civil engineering is higher than building
	s. d.	s. d.	
1938 Oct.	62 6	62 10	0·53
1948 Oct.	128 4	139 10	8·96
1958 Oct.	241 4	281 11	16·85
1959 Oct.	251 9	289 4	14·93

Table 10 shows that the percentage by which civil engineering weekly earnings are higher than building increased from 0·53 per cent to 14·93 per cent between 1938 and 1959. It might be thought that this situation can be explained quite simply by the fact that workers on civil engineering jobs put in more hours per week than those in building and that the difference is due to overtime earnings at higher rates of pay.

While it is true that more overtime is worked on civil engineering jobs the statistics indicate that this is only a marginal factor and by no means accounts entirely for the difference in earnings. The truth is that *hourly* earnings in civil engineering have gradually outstripped those in building. Taking the same 4 years as in Table 10 the position in relation to hours worked and hourly earnings is as shown in Table 11.

On earnings Table 11 shows that civil engineering workers have come from an inferiority of 1*d.* per hour in 1938 to a superiority of 4·3*d.* by 1959. Bonus earnings have obviously had a great influence on this development. Civil engineering

[6] Figures taken from table on earnings in the *Monthly Bulletin of Construction Statistics* published by the Ministry of Public Building and Works.

TABLE 11. EARNINGS AND HOURS IN BUILDING AND
CIVIL ENGINEERING

Year	Building		Civil engineering	
	Earnings: pence per hour	Hours worked per week	Earnings: pence per hour	Hours worked per week
1938 Oct.	17·3	46·1	16·3	46·6
1948 Oct.	33·0	46·6	33·8	49·6
1958 Oct.	60·1	48·2	64·2	52·7
1959 Oct.	61·7	49·0	66·0	52·6

being confined wholly to new works is relatively easy to bonus and one would expect that a large number of men operate under incentive schemes of one kind or another. A very high proportion of operatives on the building side, however, are occupied on repairs and maintenance and it is more difficult to apply bonus schemes to this type of work because much of it is non-repetitive. Workers on repairs and maintenance therefore are generally confined to the flat rate, plus whatever overtime earnings they may have. Obviously this fact is bound to reduce the overall average earnings in building compared to those in civil engineering.

Nevertheless this is only part of the story even if a significant one. Another fact is that over the years the labourer's basic rates of pay have greatly increased relative to craft rates. In February 1939, for example, the Grade "A" rate for craftsmen was 1s. 7½d. while the labourer's rate was 1s. 2¾d. By February of 1963 the respective rates were 5s. 9d. and 5s. 1½d.

While on the surface it would appear that the labourer's differential had worsened from 4¾d. in 1939 to 7½d. in 1963 it is, however, the percentage rather than the monetary differential which reveals the true position. Analysed in this way our figures show that in 1939 the labourer's rate was equal to just under 76 per cent of the craft rate; by 1963 it had increased to nearly

88 per cent of the craft rate. This situation was not to everyone's liking and various pressures arose, especially within building, with the objective of redressing the situation. Arguments that craft skill was not being adequately recompensed, and fears for the future of apprenticeship, were advanced in support of widening the differential.

And during wage negotiations in the building industry in 1965 a great deal of discussion centred round these particular points with the employers laying great emphasis on the desirability of opening the gap between the two rates. It was an argument not entirely unacceptable to some unions so, when agreement was ultimately reached between both sides, it was on the basis of a rise for all, but with craftsmen being given a larger increase sufficient to make a 1s. difference between the two rates. At March 1966 this meant standard rates of 6s. 11½d. per hour for craftsmen and 5s. 11½d. for labourers. By 1967 another "differential" increase in wage rates saw a further widening of the gap by ½d. making it 1s. 0½d. per hour.

With these changes in monetary rates the differential has widened by approximately 2 per cent so that the labourer's hourly wage is now 86 per cent of the craft rate. This is, of course, still 10 per cent improvement on the labourer's situation as compared with 1939. There is also the fact that, so long as the monetary differential remains in existence, future wage increases will inevitably bring about a reduction in the percentage differential.

The third factor which must be taken into account on earnings is the level of the various plus-rates which apply in civil engineering. Ten pages of the Working Rules of the CECCB are occupied with about 140 different plus-rates for men doing work involving extra skill, responsibility or risk, and who should therefore be paid more than the basic rate applicable to the general civil engineering operative. At least twenty-three of these rates are for amounts of 1s. 0½d. or more and this, obviously, cancels out the craft/labourer differential. Many of the other rates are only slightly below the 1s. 0½d. differential. The highest plus-rate paid is 2s. 3d. per hour for: "Driver of excavator with rated bucket capacity of 15 cu. yards." This particular operative is therefore receiving 1s 2½d. per hour more than the craft rate and his total weekly earnings are likely to be very much higher than those within building.

As civil engineering is more capital intensive than building it means a greater use of mechanization on this class of work. The result is that a large number of all civil engineering workmen will be either operating mechanical plants, or doing some related task requiring a degree of skill, for which plus-rates are in force. Irrespective of the theoretical wage differential, therefore, in practice the gap is much narrower for most men, if it is not eliminated completely.

The part that mechanization has played in replacing labour in civil engineering—at the same time as leading to increases in rates of wages for labour—has been summed up by Mr. W. G. Mitchell, who wrote:

> The extent to which mechanisation keeps costs down is not sufficiently dramatic in the short term to excite comment, but it is well illustrated by the fact that the cost of excavation to-day is on average only double what it was in the early years of the 19th Century. The contribution that mechanisation has made towards this result may be gauged from the fact that labourers' wages have risen more than 30-fold since that time.[7]

This claim about the results arising from greater use of mechanization for excavation can also be justifiably applied to other forms of civil engineering, especially road works. These developments help to explain why the civil engineering Working Rule Agreement omits any question of control on overtime. Obviously a contractor employing expensive mechanical equipment will want to exploit its full potential through overtime or three-shift working. In addition to this trend there are areas of work where normal day-shift working is difficult due to natural circumstances, such as tidal work, or like tunnelling operations where strong economic forces influence three-shift operations.

[7] In his article in the *Financial Times* Survey of Civil Engineering, 1962.

"Environmental" Factor

It is because of the special requirements of some civil engineering projects, and the more rapid introduction of mechanization and new techniques in earlier years, that the civil engineering employers wanted to be free of what they claimed was the "straight-jacket" of the building industry's working rules. They also asserted that the "environmental nature" of many of their jobs brought about a different concept of site operations not only in management but also in men, to that which existed in building.

A contractor undertaking a job such as a new hydroelectric scheme in a remote part of the country would, for example, have to face initial heavy costs in providing living accommodation and some kind of social amenities for his labour force. In addition he would need to offer wage rates which were sufficiently attractive to counter-balance the disincentive of the men having to live away from home. The contractor will have a number of reasons, therefore, for getting the job completed as soon as possible. The payment of very high earnings through "working round the clock" is then considered worth while by him if it shortens construction time and leads to large savings in his other oncosts.

To many men on such contracts this reasoning makes good sense—especially if the attractions of home are absent and they lack the general leisure facilities available in their home towns. They take the line that they may as well be working and earning instead of hanging around aimlessly. The resultant overtime on such jobs means the figures on national average overtime in construction are probably misleading because it is almost certain that men on such projects will work weekly hours far in excess of those which apply in other sections of the construction industry.

Apart from those differences between working rules based on the nature of certain operations which distinguish the civil engineering sector from building, one other difference is that the civil engineering rules provide for a faster rate of wage progression for males under the age of 18. Given that the Grade "A" labourer's rate of wage in building is the same as the Class 1 general civil engineering operative's rate, the National Working Rules for the Building Industry provide that wage progression by age for Young Male Labourers shall be:

at 15 years of age ..   .. $33\frac{1}{2}$% of adult rate
„ 16 „   „   „   ..   .. 45% „   „   „
„ 17 „   „   „   ..   .. $66\frac{2}{3}$% „   „   „
„ 18 „   „   „   ..   .. 100% „   „   „

Civil engineering, with its more immediate concern for wages paid to general operatives, lays down that the rate of progression for "Boys and Youths doing boys' and youths' work" shall be:

16–17 years ..   ..   .. 50% of the adult rate
17–18   „   ..   ..   .. 75% „   „   „   „
18 and over ..   ..   .. 100% „   „   „   „

CHAPTER 9

Wages and Conditions

National Working Rules

The building artisan of the early centuries was more independent and self-reliant—from an industrial point of view—than his modern counterpart. The client in those days was no immediate boss intent on giving detailed orders but the ultimate "owner/ occupier" who, while giving general directions about the kind of building he wanted, was then usually content to let the craftsmen proceed on the basis that they would know their own business best. And though the state, from the implementation of the Statute of Labourers in the fourteenth century, attempted to exercise control at least over wage rates the main rules governing the building worker were those laid down for his craft by the men themselves.

These were his "working rules": not imposed upon him from the top but a code of conduct which had, through time, been evolved by the men themselves in the light of their experience. To a considerable extent it was this "self-government" which give the early building worker the great pride he had in his status. And it was erosion of this self-control over job process against which he most violently rebelled in later years. The Liverpool operatives, as late as 1833, ranged themselves against the craft masters and attacked them for not having "treated our rules with that deference you ought to have done". Their long and bitter fight at that time was all part of the final losing struggle to reassert waning control over the rules which governed their conduct.

As the employers became more effectively organized the

wages and conditions applying to the industry gradually evolved as the product of joint negotiation, as in other industries. Unlike many other industries, however, the construction industry still refers to agreements on wages and conditions as the National Working Rules. This applies equally to building and to civil engineering. The basic rules are similar in both agreements but, as explained earlier, the National Working Rules for the Building Industry have been evolved over a much longer period of time and are more comprehensive. In fact, the working rules for building handbook runs to nearly 100 pages compared with less than 40 printed pages for civil engineering—and these 40 pages also include the Constitution of the Civil Engineering Conciliation Board.

Earnings in Construction

Wage rates are regarded, of course, as the most important feature around which negotiations take place. And if it is true that job status can be judged from remuneration received it is clear that the building artisan of the past was held in very high esteem. Apart from other authorities who have dealt with this matter Professor Thorold Rogers has made particular mention of the high rates paid for building craftsmen and notes that:

> at Windsor, in 1408, four carpenters got 6d. a day, and six got 5d. . . . These men were no doubt in service of the king, and the king was a very good paymaster; but he is not the only person who hires labour on these liberal terms. At York cathedral, six masons got £8 8s. a year each; six others, £7 16s.; six more £6 3s.; and one carpenter gets £7 5s. 4d.[1]

Apart from revealing that wage differentials existed even then between craftsmen—based obviously on the class of work being done—these figures also show that building workers were paid considerably higher than most others. Often they were given a food allocation in addition. For a comparison with the building rates stated by Professor Thorold Rogers there is the fact that at that time agricultural workers (when agriculture was more important in the economy of the country than it is now) were being

[1] *Six Centuries of Work and Wages*, p. 328.

paid only 4*d*. per day. Further evidence of the disparity in wage rates can also be gained from the various decisions by local magistrates when, after the Act of Elizabeth, they were given the power to regulate wages within their localities.

The magistrates meeting at Warwick in 1684 decided, for example, that skilled artisans generally should have 1*s*. a day wages, but they awarded a specially high rate of 1*s*. 4*d*. a day to the freemason. Common agricultural labourers were to have 8*d*. a day. The differential which existed between skilled artisans and agricultural labourers was, therefore, 50 per cent while the freemason had 100 per cent more.

The coming of the Industrial Revolution, and the new skills which arose as a consequence, began to lead to a comparative decline in the wage status of the building craftsman. In fact the unions have, over the years, claimed that this has been a continuing trend and their arguments for higher wages have been partly based on the need for redressing the situation. Only by working more overtime than most other industries, they state, have construction workers managed to keep abreast of the average earnings in industry generally. Is this case entirely justified? Table 12 gives the situation as it has developed from the immediate pre-war years and, so that an accurate comparison can be made, the table does not quote total weekly earnings but hours worked per week and average hourly earnings.

Table 12 shows that in 1938 average hourly earnings in construction were almost exactly the same as those in industry generally. Ten years later, however, there is a gap of 2·4*d*. per hour between them. By 1966 this monetary differential has increased to 4·2*d*. per hour. Again, however, a note of caution must be sounded on taking a too-narrow view based solely on monetary differentials. If we apply the same mathematical logic to these hourly earnings as we did earlier to the craft/labourer differentials, it reveals that the position is turning rather more in favour than against construction.

A difference of 2·4*d*. on 1948 hourly earnings of 33*d*. in construction—as against 35·4*d*. for general industry—means that

TABLE 12. HOURS WORKED AND HOURLY EARNINGS

Year as at October	Main industries including manufacturing		Construction industry*	
	Earnings: pence per hour	Hours worked per week	Earnings: pence per hour	Hours worked per week
1938	17·4	47·7	17·3	46·1
1948	35·4	46·7	33·0	46·6
1958	64·6	47·7	60·1	48·2
1961	77·7	47·4	74·1	49·4
1962	81·0	47·0	78·0	49·5
1963	84·4	47·6	80·1	49·8
1964	91·1	47·7	87·7	49·8
1965	100·0	47·0	95·3	49·8
1966	105·9	46·0	101·7	48·5

*Up to 1958 the figures relating to "Construction Industry" are those which were available for building as distinct from civil engineering contracting. After that date both categories were linked together in official statistics under the heading of "Construction".

general industrial earnings are almost 7·3 per cent higher than construction. But the money difference of 4·2d. on the higher 1966 basic figures shows that the adverse position against construction has dropped to just under 3·1 per cent, or less than half of what it was in 1948. Construction has therefore gradually reduced the gap and there are one or two major contributory factors to this situation. First there is the undeniable fact that overtime in construction has outstripped the average overtime being worked in industry generally. In 1938 weekly hours worked in construction were 1·6 below the average for industry generally. By 1966 they were 2·5 hours above. Obviously the higher premium rate on this number of extra overtime hours has helped to put up the level of hourly earnings on the whole.

Another, and more important factor was the introduction of incentive schemes for construction in 1947. Building workers had resisted the operation of incentive schemes for some years after they had been generally accepted in manufacturing industry and their earnings had accordingly suffered. Many of the building workers had objections of conscience to incentives, based on their regard for craftsmanship and consideration for their fellows on-site. Especially the older men who, they felt, "might go to the wall" if incentive schemes were introduced. By the end of the Second World War, however, the employers were trying to break down this attitude and bring in a situation where "earnings were related to productivity".

From the unions these attempts drew only hostile replies. The situation was then brought to a head in 1946 when the building unions made a claim for a sixpence-per-hour increase in basic wages. This the employers refused to consider. An arbitration tribunal which was held in the following year backed the employers and left union leaders and their members seething with anger. Many of them thought the only way they would obtain any satisfaction would be through a national strike. It was at this stage that Aneurin Bevan stepped into the ring between the contenders. As the Minister in the then Labour Government responsible for achieving housing targets which had been set, he made it clear that this was his primary objective and that he felt it necessary to use incentive schemes to achieve that end. When Bevan subsequently made an emphatic public speech along these lines it served to further inflame the unions. The Minister of Labour, now extremely apprehensive that a national strike might well take place, made his own suggestion for resolving the issue.

If the operatives would agree to the introduction of incentive schemes designed to increase their wages by around 20 per cent the employers should respond by giving a flat-rate increase of 3d. per hour. Though the employers agreed this was a reasonable compromise and were prepared to accept the Minister of Labour's recommendation, the union leaders felt the hostility of their members to incentives was such that they could not personally accept the responsibility of agreeing to the proposals. They finally decided that the only way out was to refer the matter to a national ballot of all building union members: they would have to weigh-up the attraction of the 3*d*. per hour "carrot" against the "stick" of incentives for themselves.

When the vote was taken a very high poll (compared to numbers normally participating in union ballots) of approximately 50 per cent was recorded. And the majority came down emphatically in favour of the Minister's compromise by 165,606 to 77,868. The formal introduction of incentives in the industry was then agreed to take place as from 16 November 1947.[2] In view of the fierce controversy over the initial introduction of incentives it is surprising that the total number of men in construction who are actually working genuine incentive schemes has remained very low. Ministry of Labour surveys into Payment by Results throughout the last few years have revealed that on average about 16–18 per cent of the construction industry's total labour force are covered by genuine incentive schemes.

Many employers have therefore not found it possible to get the staff necessary to administer targetted schemes, and a large number of firms may feel in any event that they are too small to justify such staff overheads. There is also the fact that a considerable amount of building work—mainly repairs and maintenance—is very difficult to bonus. On the surface, therefore, it would appear that incentives have had little effect on uplifting hourly earnings. The fact, however, is that the use of incentives by some employers has forced others, in a situation where demand for labour has generally exceeded supply, to offer straightforward plus-rates in order to compete with earnings on sites where incentive schemes operate.

As this situation has developed the negotiated basic rates have tended to become only a rough guide upon which are built various additions which sometimes result in the offer of hourly

[2] As first introduced the incentive scheme agreement carried out the Minister of Labour's suggestion of aiming at 20 per cent earnings by formally including this figure in the agreement. In later years, however, the incentive rule was revised and more detailed principles governing the operation of such schemes were laid down but no specific target of earnings was included.

rates which vary between 30 to 50 per cent above those laid down in the National Working Rules. Both employer and union organizations have, in recent years, expressed concern about this "wages drift" which has become so significant as to make negotiations on basic wage rates of almost academic importance except to the relatively small number of men who are confined by the circumstances of their employment to negotiated rates.

Basic Wage Rates

The basic, negotiated rates of wages, as at July 1967, were as shown in Table 13.

TABLE 13. HOURLY WAGE RATES

Building trade				Civil engineering			
London and Liverpool		Grade A		London and Liverpool		Grade A	
Crafts-men	Labour-ers	Crafts-men	Labour-ers	Crafts-men	General opera-tives	Crafts-men	General opera-tives
7s. 5½d.	6s. 5d.	7s. 4d.	6s. 3½d.	7s. 5½d.	6s. 5d.	7s. 4d.	6s. 3½d.

Having earlier considered the factors influencing total earnings in the industry we now turn to the three which, in particular, have brought about increases in the negotiated basic rates. The first is that the basic rate has been altered from time to time by joint negotiation. Secondly, all those workers in the lower-graded areas (as mentioned in Chapter 7, there used to be seventeen different grades with a differing rate applying in each) have had their rates effectively boosted as all the grades below Grade A were gradually eliminated by union pressure. Thirdly, the 1921 joint agreement provided for automatic variation in the basic rate according to movements in the Index of Retail Prices under what is known in the industry as the Sliding Scale Agreement (SSA).

Though the immediate years after 1921 saw a drastic reduction in wage rates due to the depression which led to a lowering of the Index of Retail Prices figure, the general inflationary environment in the post-war period has led to an automatic rise in rates in most years due to the SSA. This rule provides that in each year the average movement in the Index of Retail Prices over the past 12 months will be calculated, and that wage rates will alter by $\frac{1}{2}d$. for each two-point move in the Index up or down according to the way in which prices have moved.

The SSA was not, however, as some had hoped the complete answer to protracted wrangling over wage rates. The unions asserted that increases under the SSA could not always fully meet their claims. They pointed out, for instance, that the SSA increase was always awarded a year later than the period over which it had been calculated: it therefore never met the current price position. Their major argument, however, was that even assuming the SSA satisfactorily provided for increases in prices it never led to a rise in real wages. The logical consequence of this reasoning was that the unions continued to make claims for increases in basic rates even though these were being constantly adjusted due to awards under the SSA. In fact it is the negotiations on basic wage rates which have secured the greater part of the total increase which has taken place, while the SSA awards have provided only a supplement. From 1960 to July 1967, for example, the Grade A craft rate rose from 4s. $10\frac{1}{2}d$. to 7s. 4d. SSA increases accounted for $6\frac{1}{2}d$., or about 22 per cent of the total.

In recent years the employers have looked with growing disfavour upon the SSA. Not only had it failed to obviate the need to spend many months of almost every year arguing over claims for wage increases; it also became an obstacle to their desire for long-term wage agreements providing for specified increases over a period of about 3 years. Obviously wage agreements of this kind would be of particular assistance to construction employers in view of the contractual nature of the industry; it is of great value in making up a tender for a job if it is known what the basic rates of pay will be throughout the life of the project. In 1963 the employers therefore managed to persuade the unions to agree the first "package deal" setting out specified dates upon which basic increases were to be given. No attempt was then made to suggest termination of the SSA, although it obviously left a loop-hole whereby wage increases of an unknown quantity might still take place irrespective of the long-term agreement.

When this first package deal came to an end, however, the most contentious discussions about the terms of the next one centred upon the employers insistence that the SSA should now finish. In these discussions the unions were, to a considerable extent, at some disadvantage. For while the employers were apparently unanimous in their desire to end the SSA, the union side was less united in defence of the agreement. There were some who had previously criticized it for its ineffectiveness but who now found it possessed admirable qualities and pressed for its retention. Other union spokesmen claimed that the SSA was responsible for only a small increase in any one year and that this increase was subsequently wielded by the employers as a weapon to attack union claims for more important basic wage improvements. They thought, on balance, they were better without it.

With unanimity on one side, and divided opinion on the other, it was almost inevitable that conclusions on the 1965 negotiations should provide for the end of the Sliding Scale Agreement as from February 1968, after 48 years of existence. The terms of the 1965 settlement adding that after termination of the SSA: "When determining the standard rate of wages in consequent years the Council shall have regard (inter-alia) to the need to safeguard the Parties from the consequence of sharp and unforeseen fluctuations in the cost of living."

Apprenticeship

In addition to setting down basic wage rates for adult operatives the National Working Rules also define those applying to craft apprentices; young male labourers (details given in the last chapter); for the relatively few women workers in the industry who are normally employed in factories, and also certain "Extra Payments" for men doing work which involves "Discomfort, Inconvenience or Risk" or the exercise of "Continuous Extra Skill or Responsibility" or of "Intermittent Responsibility". Some of these latter plus-rates are similar in amount to those laid down in the Civil Engineering Working Rules Agreement. Unlike that agreement however, which concentrates on extra rates based largely on the labourers' position, the National Working Rules for the Building Industry also include "Extra Payments" for the craftsmen doing work coming under the heading of the various categories.

The wage for apprentices in the industry is expressed as a percentage of the adult craft rate according to the age of the apprentice. The scale is:

Age 15 ..	..	One-quarter
„ 16 ..	..	One-third
„ 17 ..	..	One-half
„ 18 ..	..	Five-eighths
„ 19 ..	..	Three-quarters
„ 20 ..	..	Seven-eighths

The full adult rate is paid on completion of apprenticeship where this takes place "on or after the 20th birthday, and in any event at the age of 21". And although six different rates are stated, "the normal period of indentured apprenticeship is prescribed to be four years beginning not earlier than the apprentice's 16th birthday". The 15-year-old wage rate provides for school-leavers of that age who enter the industry with a view to taking up apprenticeship at the prescribed age.

One point about the 4 years' apprenticeship which should be noted is that, although unions and employers in construction have been accused of having a reactionary outlook on such matters, it was the first major industry to reduce the normal

period of apprenticeship to 4 years. Because it was a rather enterprising step at the time, which might not have been universally
approved, the agreement was at first in the form of "permissive
legislation" allowing those regional joint councils which wished
to do so to reduce the apprenticeship period. This regional
approach allowed the principle to be established where both
employers and unions desired it, without the necessity of fighting
to overcome the resistance which was evident in certain parts of
the country.

In course of time the establishment of a shorter apprenticeship
in some regions, bordering on others which maintained the 5-year
period, was rightly recognized as leading to an absurd situation.
And as from the 5 April 1965 it was agreed that the 4-year
apprenticeship be generally applied throughout Britain. At the
same time the apprenticeship rules as a whole were made much
less rigid in that regional joint apprenticeship committees (or
local committees where such authority was delegated to them)
can now at their discretion allow youths into apprenticeship
at a later age than 16 "provided that a minimum period of three
years is served and the apprenticeship does not end earlier than
the apprentice's 21st birthday".

The National Joint Apprenticeship Scheme for the building
industry is an admirable one which seeks to safeguard the interests of the apprentice and ensure that he receives sound training.
The serious loophole which still exists is that many boys are not
protected by formal indentures but take up their apprenticeship
purely on verbal assurances which have almost no standing in
law. At one time the proportion of "verbal" apprenticeships
formed the majority. Gradually the situation bettered until by
1962 a national survey showed that 44,600 apprentices out of a
total of 78,200 were officially indentured. Since then the position
has further improved and the establishment of the Construction
Industry's Training Board should lead ultimately to a situation
where almost 100 per cent of the apprentices are formally indentured.

Wage Rates for Females

When thinking of apprenticeship it is almost always in terms of young males: few women work in the industry outside of the professional, technical or clerical grades. Nevertheless, there are a number of females employed on certain skilled processes and there are also women engaged on duties which make them the equivalent of a general labourer. For these female workers National Working Rule 1(k) of the Building Industry lays down the following rates:

FEMALE OPERATIVES

(i) The standard rate for women aged 19 and over engaged on craft processes shall be 85 per cent of the current Grade "A" standard rate for craftsmen.

(ii) The standard rate for women aged 19 and over engaged on work other than craft processes shall be 85 per cent of the current Grade "A" standard rate for labourers.

(iii) Probationers (19 or over) on craft processes (period of probation 6 months).

First Month ⎰
Second Month ⎱ 4*d.*
Third Month ⎰
Fourth Month ⎱ 3*d.*   per hour below the standard Rate for Women in (i) above
Fifth Month ⎰
Sixth Month ⎱ 2*d.*

(iv) Girls and Young Women under 19:
Aged 15—33½ per cent of the Standard Rate for Women in (i) above
„ 16—45   „   „   „   „   „   „   „   „
„ 17—66⅔ „   „   „   „   „   „   „   „
„ 18—80   „   „   „   „   „   „   „   „

Working Hours

Apart from wages the major point of negotiating pressure by the building unions has been to obtain a shortening of basic working hours per week. It would not be an exaggeration to claim that building operatives have, for most of the time during which unions have existed, taken a lead in industrial struggle to cut weekly working hours. During the strike begun by the Operative Builders Union in 1833 (dealt with in Chapter 3) one of the demands of the men, which had originated in the mind of Robert Owen, was for an 8-hour day. In the social and economic environment of that time this claim was as wildly visionary as some of the other principles which the men propounded—almost a century in fact before their time. And though this objective was not then realized Raymond Postgate claimed that: "The operatives . . . never forgot this lesson, that the best aim they could have was a genuine shortening of hours, and from this date onwards the exclusive preoccupation about contracting and minor working rules tends to give way to the far more important question of hours."[3]

The building workers subsequently showed their concern for cutting working hours by a series of long-drawn-out strikes aimed at reducing them from 10 to 9 hours a day. By 1853 the London area unions had also set up joint organizations with this object in view. When they first petitioned one or two employers on the matter the men themselves were rather amazed to find that, without need for industrial strife, the Crystal Palace Company "gave them this boon". But the reaction of other employers, when they heard of this, was such that they hardened their attitude against reducing working hours and it was only after a number of bitter disputes that any significant reduction in hours was gained in 1872. Even then they were far from uniform throughout the country (no national agreement existed to make the position otherwise) and the London masons came off best with an average working week of 51 hours: "The $52\frac{1}{2}$-hour week worked during 40 weeks of the year is compensated for by 47 hours per week worked in the 12 winter weeks."[4]

This lack of uniformity continued for many years throughout the industry and even in 1918 it was shown that Liverpool bricklayers were working an average week of $46\frac{1}{2}$ hours in the main

[3] *The Builders' History*, p. 97.
[4] *OSM Returns*, 4 July 1872.

summer months, reducing to 44 in the autumn and then down to $41\frac{1}{2}$ in the winter while, at the other end of the scale, the brick-layers were working hours which averaged out to 55 per week throughout the year. It was into this situation that the newly formed National Federation of Building Trades Operatives, in 1918, made a claim for weekly working hours to be reduced to 44. The unity with which the unions put forward their claim through the Federation was, however, matched by that of the employers in rejecting it. The matter was then referred to the National Board of Conciliation.

As this meant another confrontation of much the same union and employer leaders it was not surprising that the result was again stalemate on the NBC. After further deadlock the acrimo-nious debates were adjourned to a meeting of the Board scheduled for September 1919. At this meeting hours of debate took place without the parties coming to a decision, and it looked as if only a trial of strength would resolve the situation. To bring an end to formalities the unions finally made a stand by moving: "That the 44 hour week come into operation as from 1 May 1920." But instead of the anticipated deadlocked voting the unions were both astonished and delighted when two employers crossed their votes to support them. They had actually achieved a long-cherished ideal without the necessity of having to battle for it on the sites.

The general economic collapse which took place almost immediately after, however, made all the gains of the previous years as haphazard as a game of snakes and ladders. The unions had reached a standard of wages and conditions which was now seriously threatened. In fact the employers first managed to bring about a number of wage reductions and then moved to the next step of threatening that, to meet the challenge of the depression, it would be necessary to increase the basic working hours per week. This was a more serious threat to the unions than the fall in wages. They therefore met the Trades Union Congress leaders and Labour Members of Parliament for urgent discussions and, having gained promises of support, made plans for a national strike. And it was only after the then Leader of the Labour Party,

Ramsay MacDonald, managed to persuade both union and employer leaders to talk with him at the House of Commons that conflict was averted and the matter brought to arbitration.

Sir Hugh Fraser, the appointed arbitrator, studied the position and then made two separate awards. It was his second one which dealt with the question of working hours. He awarded that, as from the 17 September 1923, hours should be increased to 46½ per week in the summer with 44 still applying in the winter months. He added, however, that in any town or district where agreement could be jointly obtained to continue the 44-hour week this should be maintained. Obviously the award was not seen by the unions as calculated to cool the passions of the operatives and, in effect, seemed more like a recipe for further strikes. The proposal that the 44-hour week might still apply "where agreement could be jointly obtained" was almost tantamount, thought the unions, to saying: "where the men are sufficiently strong to enforce the *status quo* on the employers."

Succeeding years therefore saw constant negotiations and disputes over the diverse pattern of hours being worked throughout the country. Gradually, however, the unions managed to eliminate the 46½-hour week in the summer from one district after another until by October 1960 a universal 44-hour week applied throughout the country. And this was the moment chosen by the union negotiators, led by veteran Federation Secretary Sir Richard Coppock, to press a claim for an even shorter basic working week. They succeeded in their objective and gained an agreement that the 42-hour week should apply as from October 1961. But even this rate of progress lagged behind the ambitions of the rank and file membership, and conferences of the various unions were already calling for a really significant break-through to the 40-hour working week.

In Scotland, which had long been a pioneer in the struggle for shorter hours, the operatives decided on a unilateral attempt to gain this objective. After a short trial of strength with the Scottish Employers "the prize" was theirs as from 4 November 1963. One automatic result was, of course, a disparity in hours and wage rates between Scotland and the rest of the country. Another was that the operatives in England and Wales immediately urged their union leaders to press for application of the 40-hour week throughout the rest of Great Britain.

Though the employers probably accepted that the break-through in Scotland must inevitably be realized in England and Wales they nevertheless refused to concede immediately. Only after prolonged negotiations leading to the package deal of November 1965 was it agreed that the 40-hour week apply in England and Wales as from Monday, 7 March 1966. As a part of this agreement compensatory increases in basic wage rates were given to offset the reduction in hours, and in Scotland a slight wage adjustment was also made so that weekly working hours and the standard rates of wages would be the same throughout Great Britain.

The operatives had hoped that, with the introduction of the 40-hour week, it would be worked in 5 days. However, the employers insisted that there was a good case for allowing them discretion to work a $5\frac{1}{2}$-day week during the mid-winter period in order to maximize daylight working. Reluctantly the unions had to accept this and National Working Rule 2 on Working Hours now reads:

1. Normal Working Hours.

   The normal working hours shall be 40 per week throughout the year, to be worked in five days—Mondays to Fridays, 8 hours per day.

   During the mid-winter period of six weeks before and six weeks after Christmas, the normal weekly working hours may, at the Employer's option, be worked in five and a half days, in which case the daily hours to be worked at plain time rates shall be:

Mondays to Thursdays	..	..	..	$7\frac{1}{4}$ hours
Fridays	..	..	..	7 hours
Saturdays	..	..	..	4 ,,

2. Meal Intervals.

   In all cases there shall be a break or breaks for refreshment at a time or times to be fixed by arrangement between the employer and operatives at each site, job or shop. The breaks which shall not exceed one hour per day in aggregate, shall include a dinner interval of not less than half-an-hour.

3. Starting Times.

   The actual time of starting work shall be as determined and published by the Local Joint Committee: provided that by arrangement between the employer and the operatives on a site, job or in a shop the starting time for that site, job or shop may be advanced by not more than half-an-hour, and provided always that in no case shall normal working hours start earlier than 7.30 a.m.

Holidays With Pay

One of the greatest advances in working conditions during the twentieth century has been the widespread achievement of holidays with pay. Though paid holidays are now accepted as an automatic and important part of working conditions throughout industry, it is only in comparatively recent years that the principle was finally consolidated into practice. Though a few adventurous leaders were urging, just after the turn of the century, that there should be a fight for the "great boon" of paid holidays it was only in a few industries that this had been implemented up to the beginning of the Second World War (in engineering, for example, the first agreement on holidays was made in 1937). Such agreements as were made generally laid down that 1 week's paid holiday would be granted to workers who had put in about a full year's service with a particular employer.

One reason for the general delay in implementing paid holidays was that the inter-war years of depressed economic conditions hardly provided the basis from which the unions could proceed from propaganda to positive action in support of their demands. But with the start of the Second World War the ranks of the unemployed began to melt and union leaders found themselves in an increasingly stronger position to press claims, and paid holidays were gradually extended to an ever wider section of workers.

In construction, however, the unions recognized that it was not employer reluctance which provided the only obstacle to holidays with pay. The excessively casual nature of employment was almost as great a barrier. No employer could be expected to give a man paid holidays unless he had been with the firm for a reasonable time. Yet the contractual nature of the industry meant that many workers might change their employment several times in any one

year. The men in construction, therefore, witnessed the introduction of paid holidays in other industries but were only too aware
that an apparently insurmountable barrier lay between themselves
and a similar objective. Then, in 1942, a simple if ingenuous
solution was found. The obstacle of casual employment would be
overcome by issuing to each man, at the start of a specified
"payment year", a card on which would be affixed a holiday
credit stamp by his employer for every week he worked for him.

Even if he did have a number of different employers during the
year they would, by giving him stamps, be providing their proportion of his holiday pay for the following year's "holiday
period". The method of operation conceived was simple in that
employers purchased stamps from the head office of the Holidays
With Pay Scheme during the "payment year", and the office in
the following year paid out cash to the value of the stamps on each
card returned to it in respect of an operative taking his annual
holidays.

The agreement reached on 28 October 1942 provided that
holiday stamps would be issued as from the 1 February 1943.
This agreement was also notable because it necessitated the coming
together of the building and civil engineering joint councils in
order to make a four-party agreement ratifying the scheme. In the
normal way it had not been necessary for the two councils to
come together for the implementation of any of the agreements
they made in relation to their own sectors of the construction
industry. With the advent of the Holidays With Pay Scheme,
however, a new office administration had to be set up and a
controlling board appointed. This could only be accomplished by
all of the parties joining together to make a common agreement
distinct from the working rules separately negotiated by their
normal joint council machinery.

The Holidays With Pay Scheme is therefore an agreement
signed by the four major parties in the construction industry:
the National Federation of Building Trade Employers; the
National Federation of Building Trades Operatives; the Federation of Civil Engineering Contractors and the Operatives' Panel

of the Civil Engineering Conciliation Board. On the Board which controls the policy and administration of the Holidays With Pay Scheme there are 12 directors, nominated from the organizations which are party to the agreement, together with an independent chairman.

Responsible to the Board for the actual administration of the Scheme, which takes place in a large, modern office block at Crawley, are officials and staff for whom a total wages and salary bill of over £255,000 per year is incurred. Dealing with most of the firms in the construction industry, and covering annually up to one million operatives, the turnover of the Scheme each year runs into many millions of pounds.

For the year ending 31 March 1966, for example, nearly 74 million stamps were issued worth almost £29 million. Obviously a large income is needed to pay for administration of the Scheme and it was decided that a small charge should be levied on each holiday card to pay for expenses of administration. However, the amount raised in this way has, over the years, become increasingly insufficient to meet expenditure. For the year ending 31 March 1966, the total amount raised from the administration charge came to only £86,418—which was not anything like enough to pay that year's total expenses of £556,709. The gap between income and expenditure is, however, met by the revenue from investment of money paid for stamps.

As the income from stamps sales is received over the year, previous to the year in which it is paid out, the sum collected is available for investment. For the year 1966 the revenue from this source alone came to over £1,305,000, which boosted the total income to over £1,406,000. After tax payments of approximately £543,000 on the investment income, and meeting total administrative expenses, there was a surplus for the year amounting to nearly £307,000.

The financial turnover of the Scheme would be even greater if all construction workers were covered for full holiday entitlements. Each operative in the industry is allowed a total of 3 weeks holiday (2 weeks annual holiday and the other made up of public holidays) and holiday stamp credits are aimed at providing them with holiday pay equivalent to a basic week's wages for each week of holidays. If all operatives participated in the scheme the total turnover in stamps might be upwards of £50 million. However, a number of construction workers are covered by holiday arrangements established by the firms which employ them. There are also a large number of men who are so casually employed in construction that they only collect a few holiday credits during any one year. In addition apprentices are outwith the scope of the Holiday Scheme because, as they are normally indentured to a particular employer for the whole period of their apprenticeship, he is responsible for payment of their holidays.

A slight anomaly that originally arose for apprentices is that, with employers paying for holidays, during their first year as fully trained craftsmen they did not have any stamps to their credit when taking holidays that year. The Scheme now provides that throughout the last year of apprenticeship an annual holiday card and a public holidays card shall be provided for the apprentice, and stamps will be affixed on the card so that during his first year as an adult craftsman he will be able to draw holiday pay through the Scheme.

The present holidays specified for construction workers define that: "Each operative covered by the scheme shall be granted two weeks' of annual holidays not necessarily in continuity." These 2 weeks have to be taken during the summer period which is between 1 April to 31 October in each year. Generally the first week of annual holiday is decided by the employer, after consultation with his operatives, so that a mutually convenient date can be arranged to apply at a particular works or site.

The date of the second week of annual holiday is decided by the employer who then has to notify his operatives of this date "as soon as possible but, in any event, no less than 28 days" before the date of the holiday.

In relation to public holidays the rule specifies that: "In each locality there shall be not less than 5 days of public holiday in each year additional to Christmas Day." It can be seen that the holiday rules are framed to fit contractual operations in the industry and also to allow for the various localities determining the time at which they will have their own holidays.

There have been objections to the present rules by operatives on the grounds that many of them wish to have their fortnight's holiday concurrently rather than in two separate weeks. There is also resentment that, for the second week of holiday, the employer has the right to decide when it should be taken—subject only to having to give his men a minimum of 28 days notice of the date decided upon. The operatives claim, with some justification, that this arrangement leaves them with little possibility of making advance travel and accommodation arrangements.

Nevertheless, with these reservations, the advent of holidays with pay in the construction industry was a very great advance for the workers. Credit must also be given to those responsible for the detailed management of the Scheme because it commenced in 1942 literally on the basis of one man sharing a part of office accommodation. It is therefore sound administration from the first, allied to shrewd investment of money, which has resulted in the present efficient head office which is unique for its application of mechanization to the requirements of the Scheme. It is certainly the most advanced administration of its kind in Europe. The success of the Scheme has turned the minds of certain leaders in the industry towards the possibility of further exploiting its potential (an outline of the way in which this might be done is given in the next chapter).

Sickness and Injury Pay

One idea which has been implemented in recent years is the provision, under National Working Rule 9, of payment for absence due to sickness or injury. Under National Working Rule 9 all adult operatives in construction, male or female, are entitled to sickness or injury benefit for a total period of 48 days during any one year—the year being taken as the accounting period for the Holidays With Pay Scheme.

To qualify for benefit the operative must have, in the period of 8 weeks before the sickness or injury period commences, at least four weekly credit stamps on his annual holidays card. The card issued for the Holidays With Pay Scheme therefore acts as an effective qualification for entitlement to sickness or injury benefit. In this way these benefits have been introduced almost without additional administrative costs being incurred by the industry.

Under National Working Rule 9 the operative is entitled, if absent from work on account of sickness or injury, to the sum of 10s. per working day. He must satisfy his employer that the incapacity is genuine through a certificate issued by a registered medical practitioner. No payment, however, is made for the first 3 days of each period of absence. Nor do Sundays or the days of annual or public holidays count for payment.

The whole sickness and injury payment scheme is effectively controlled by the Holidays With Pay card because, apart from stamps on the card qualifying the operative to receive benefit, the card also contains a number of spaces to provide for employers keeping a record of the amount of sickness or accident payments made to operatives.

Termination of Employment

When the building unions fought their bitter and unsuccessful battles to retain day wages—as opposed to the employers objective of bringing in hourly rates of pay—it was because they feared that hourly wages would inevitably lead to hire and fire on the same basis. The industry, unfortunately, has too long been associated with a ruthless reputation in this respect. Improvement of the situation has only come about in comparatively recent years, with conditions of service and notice to terminate employment being brought more into line with industry generally.

National Working Rule 2B now specifies that notice to terminate employment, from either the employer or operative, is that during the first 6 normal working days of employment 2 hours' notice can be given to expire at the end of normal working hours on any day. After the first 6 working days, however, 1 clear day's notice must be given and this expires at the end of normal working hours on a Friday. Before looking at the other periods of notice it should be noted that this means, in effect, a man could have between 1 day's notice and almost a week. If his employer became disgruntled with him on the Monday, for example, and gave him notice it would still not apply until the end of normal working hours on the Friday giving him almost the whole week. If, however, the disaffection took place on the Thursday evening there would still be time for the employer to give him the one clear day's notice to expire at the end of the Friday working day.

The rule goes on to specify that after 26 weeks' continuous employment 7 clear days' notice must be given to terminate employment. With the passing of the Contracts of Employment Act, 1963, statutory requirements have now supplemented these particular provisions so that after 2 years' continuous employment 2 weeks' notice is required and, after 5 years' continuous employment, 4 weeks' notice must be given. Although workers throughout industry generally welcomed the Contracts of Employment Act as an advance in their conditions the unions in the construction industry made it clear that they considered the Act to have little relevance to construction workers. Very few operatives, they claimed, have anything like 2 years' continuous work in employment with any single employer. And only a handful of staff or "key men" have anything approaching 5 years' continuous employment. The higher periods of notice specified in the Contracts of Employment Act will, therefore, have little significance for construction workers.

National Working Rule 2B also specifies that in cases of misconduct an operative may be summarily discharged at any time. Another qualification in the Rule is based very much on the industry's methods of operation and this is that: "In the exceptional case where work is stopped upon the instructions of a recognised competent authority, the employer shall be free to terminate the Operative's employment at one clear day's notice to expire at the end of normal working hours on any day."

The changing location of sitework is also recognized and the Rule gives employers the discretion to transport an operative from one job to another.

In addition to laying down the various periods of notice required to terminate employment the Rule states that: "the contract of employment shall be deemed a contract from hour to hour and payments other than the payments prescribed under National Working Rules 2A and 9 [for inclement weather and sickness or injury] shall be for time actually worked."

Guaranteed Time

A major grievance of men in the construction industry is that they are—more than any other class of worker—likely to suffer loss of earnings due to inclement weather. The unions also claim that, even if the twice-yearly surveys on industrial earnings by the Ministry of Labour showed construction operatives to have about the general level, their total earnings will still probably be lower because of time and earnings lost beyond their control. This is an old complaint and one of the early National Working Rules was to make provision for compensating operatives for earnings lost under such circumstances. There is also the fact that, quite apart from the incidence of inclement weather, site production might cease due to non-arrival of materials or other similar causes.

While the first agreement on compensatory payments for time lost was valuable in that it established the vital principle involved, it was unsatisfactory to the operatives in that total "make-up pay" was much less than the basic weekly wage. Negotiations over the years between the two sides have therefore aimed at resolving this and other objections by establishing a system much fairer to the operatives. The current National Working Rule 2A dealing with "Time Lost Through Causes Beyond the Control of the Parties" now lays down a guaranteed weekly minimum of 36 hours (still 4 hours' less than the basic working week) and also improved entitlement to the guarantee.

To qualify for payment under this rule an operative has to

present himself for work each day and remain available for work throughout the normal working hours. Decision as to when work is to be carried out, interrupted and resumed, lies with the "employer or his representative and shall be implicitly observed". Where an operative has complied with this requirement:

> but during any part of that week has been prevented from working by reason of inclement weather, plant breakdown, non-arrival of materials or other similar causes beyond the control of the parties—
>
> (a) he shall receive payment at his current hourly rate for half the time lost by him on that account during his normal working hours;
>
> (b) his total payment in respect of (i) normal working hours worked in that week, and (ii) any payments under 2 (a) above shall together be not less than 36 times the hourly wage rate applicable to him in that week (this amount being referred to hereinafter as the "guaranteed weekly minimum").

In effect, the Rule provides that an operative receives a minimum of 36 hours' pay at basic rates even if severe weather has prevented him from working at all in any week. On the other hand he may have worked 30 hours and been prevented by inclement weather from completing his normal weekly hours and, in this event, he receives compensatory payment of 6 hours.

One accusation made by operatives was that employers would try if possible to avoid being responsible for payment of guaranteed time if no work was at all possible due to bad weather. At one union conference a delegate alleged that, in his region, some employers had made a practice of phoning up the meteorological office during the winter—near the end of a week—to find out what the weather was likely to be in the ensuing week. If the report was that frost or snow was expected the employer would make use of the Rule on termination of employment on Fridays in order to discharge his men and evade paying them guaranteed time the following week.

To meet this objection from the unions it was agreed that a new clause 3 in Rule 2A should apply specifying that:

> Where work is temporarily stopped (e.g. through inclement weather) and a pay-week in which the operative actually works is followed immediately by a complete pay-week during which although remaining available

for work throughout, he is prevented from performing actual work, he shall be entitled to the guaranteed minimum weekly payment for that second week.

Of course, even the unions appreciate that, while the employer will have added a sum to his contract tender figure to cover expected non-productive time, he could not possibly continue to carry men through a prolonged bad spell of weather. National Working Rule 2A therefore adds that, after the terms of clause 3 have been met, the operative may be required by the employer to register as an unemployed person.

It is always difficult to set down rules governing payments of this kind, which particularly affect an industry like construction, but the terms of the Rules can now be said to provide reasonable compensatory payment for the operatives. There are still gaps in the provisions, of course, and one stated aim of the unions affiliated to the National Federation of Building Trade Operatives is to obtain a guaranteed week of 40 hours and that it should apply throughout the year.

Union Stewards

Although union stewards have been a feature of construction sites for very many years it is only recently that they, and their functions, were given an official place in the National Working Rules. The previous reluctance by many employers to define their official status in this way reflected a rather shortsighted outlook. Certainly the employers may have had their suspicions about union stewards arising from the irresponsible conduct of a few stewards mainly active in certain areas of the country. But this should not have blurred the fact that there are many hundreds of stewards doing a sound and responsible job which, in the long run, has a beneficial effect on keeping site operations moving smoothly.

The employers also failed to understand that the aggressive steward, who built up a personal following sufficient to enable him to act independently of his union, and often rashly, was more of a danger to union leaders for it was their immediate authority which was being challenged and undermined. As long as nothing was laid down in the Working Rules defining the authority and functions of a steward the unions were relatively powerless to suppress a steward who held meetings, or token strikes, in support of political or other matters which were irrelevant to his real responsibilities in relation to the Working Rules. It was therefore of benefit to both sides to have his duties formally defined.

After a series of discussions between the employers and unions it was finally agreed to establish National Working Rule 7 relating to the "Recognition of Union Representatives". The Rule states that:

> A site, job or shop steward who has been appointed in accordance with the rules of the union, has been duly accredited by the union and has been in the employment of the employer for six working days, shall, upon written notification by the union to the employer of his appointment, be recognised as the representative of the members of that union employed at the site, job or shop.

The functions of the stewards are laid down in clause 4 of the Rule which affirms that the primary purpose of the steward is to:

> represent the workmen concerned, to investigate any complaint or difficulties arising, to approach management thereon as necessary and generally to co-operate with management to ensure that the Working Rule Agreement is observed by both parties.

In order that the stewards are able to carry out these duties the management has to give reasonable facilities to them while the steward, in return, is not to abuse the facilities. For instance, the Rule emphatically states that: "Stewards shall not leave their place of work to conduct union business without the permission of management, and then only to conduct such business as is urgent and relevant to the site, job or shop."

The employers have in the past aired their grievance about the amount of time claimed by some of the stewards as essential for carrying out their duties. Some of them were also given to calling meetings of the men at times decided by themselves. To meet these objections the Rule therefore adds that no meetings of workmen shall be held during working hours except with the prior permission of the management, nor can inspection of trade union-membership cards take place during working hours unless the management also agrees.

The Rule in relation to stewards, being of recent origin, is capable of further refinement in covering the relationships of stewards and site management. It is generally agreed, however, that the important advance was in obtaining agreement on the basic essentials and to have them introduced into the National Working Rules.

Labour-only Sub-contracting

One of the greatest post-war controversies in construction has centred round the rapid growth of labour-only sub-contracting. The system itself is generally thought to be the product of a continuing labour shortage in the industry, and of the desire by operatives to maximize their earnings. Also, when employer responsibilities for payments such as training levy, redundancy pay, began to increase it spurred the development of labour-only sub-contractors—especially on a self-employed basis.

Union hostility to this trend based itself on a number of factors. They claimed that labour-only workers were inclined to have no regard for the National Working Rules or any other agreements, such as the Holidays With Pay Scheme, aimed at bringing greater order and efficiency to an industry badly in need of these qualities. Labour-only sub-contractors were also often "men of straw" who left members of their gang in the lurch because they were unable to pay them. Operatives working for them who met with accident, or death, frequently were not covered by insurance and their families suffered as a consequence. There was also a genuine union feeling that a lot of the work produced by labour-only workers was of a poor quality and therefore a bad reflection on the industry.

The union which found itself most affected was the Amalgamated Union of Building Trade Workers (AUBTW). It reacted initially by trying to outlaw labour-only from the sites and refusing to accept into membership those operatives who worked under the system. The motives of the AUBTW were certainly genuine in that its Executive Council and full-time officers felt they were fighting against something which menaced the well-being of the operatives as well as the industry's reputation. But the AUBTW's efforts were, at best, only partly successful and labour-only gradually spread throughout bricklaying and then increasingly affected other trades.

The matter having gone beyond the concern of one union became something which had to be thrashed out through the NFBTO. In the subsequent discussions which took place it was evident that there was internal conflict about the best method of tackling the problem. The view of some unions that labour-only was a fact of industrial life—and control should be gained over it so that its most disturbing consequences were alleviated—clashed with the attitude of those who felt that an all-out effort should be waged to kill labour-only completely. The final result, though still fiercely opposed by the AUBTW, was the decision to agree with the employers that a new National Working Rule (No. 8) should be set-up to cover "Sub-contracting for Labour Only". It states:

> The employment on a site by a main contractor of a sub-contractor for labour-only is subject to the following conditions:
> 1. That the main contractor shall require the labour-only sub-contractor to observe, and the sub-contractor shall observe, the Working Rule Agreement and the decisions of the National Joint Council.
> 2. That in the event of a default by the labour-only sub-contractor, the main contractor shall accept responsiblity for:
>   (a) wages at the standard rate due (but not paid) to the sub-contractor's operatives in respect of time worked on the site during the pay week immediately prior to the default, plus any time worked in the pay week in which the default occurs; and
>   (b) annual and public holidays credit stamps which should have, but have not, been affixed to the cards of the sub-contractor's operatives during the period of their employment on the site.
> 3. The main contractor shall satisfy himself that the operatives employed by the labour-only sub-contractor are covered by a current employer's liability insurance policy.
> 4. The labour-only sub-contractor shall afford the same facilities for access of trade union officers as are afforded by the main contractor.

Though the Rule apparently covers the major points of concern its adoption has not (at least from the union point of view) helped ease the conflict over labour-only. In certain respects it has intensified it because of the way in which different interpretations are placed on it. The unions insist their conception of the Rule is that it is in the nature of an insurance policy. Where labour-only is apparently unavoidable then the operatives, under the Rule, at least have minimum guarantees. The unions add that, nevertheless, they always favour employers directly employing operatives and under the full terms of the National Working Rules.

They express resentment that, contrary to their understanding of the motives underlying agreement on Rule 8, some employers have taken it to imply the legalizing of labour-only sub-contracting. Allegations have also been made that, after ratification of the Rule, some directly employed operatives were sacked and replaced by labour-only sub-contractors and this led to disputes. The unions also claim that, on certain large jobs which have been opened up subsequently, contractors have made no attempt to obtain labour direct but have given out large areas of work to labour-only sub-contractors. When challenged on this point the main contractors use the Rule as a shield for their actions. The impasse which conflicting views can lead to was seen in the classic legal case of the *AUBTW* v. *Emerald Construction Company* when the union tried to insist on the main contractor using only directly employed labour for brickwork.

Rule 8 has therefore not solved one of the most vexed problems in the construction industry today. So wide is the concern which has recently been expressed over labour-only sub-contracting that the matter has figured on a number of occasions on the floor of the House of Commons. One direct result is that the Minister of Labour has set up the Phelps–Brown Committee which is currently investigating the effect on the industry of labour-only sub-contracting and is inviting evidence from all interested organizations. It may be that the Phelps–Brown Committee will produce a report which can be used as a basis for achieving a better understanding between employers and unions over labour-only sub-contracting.

Certainly the Committee is taking its terms of reference very seriously. Apart from inviting written and oral evidence from all those concerned with the problem, it initiated, in September 1967, an extremely thorough research project on the employment of labour in construction. Carrying out the project is Research Services Ltd. who will be interviewing 1000 construction firms and 115 local authorities. The survey will aim at finding out the extent to which firms maintain a permanent labour force, how far they rely on casual labour and labour-only workers and what their experiences are of this type of labour.

The project may well be one of the most rewarding ever carried out in construction. Certainly it should produce hard evidence as against the present surmise on which is based much of the acrimony over labour-only. It is expected that the report of the Phelps–Brown Committee, and of the special survey, should be ready some time in 1968.

Industrialized Building

In addition to the formal Working Rules which, apart from the ones already referred to, go on to deal with Tool Allowances, Travelling Time and other matters of detail, the book containing the Rules also has within its pages a number of agreements on other matters. The most important of these are the ones which relate to Industrialization of Building Processes and the setting out of the General Principles concerning Incentive Schemes.

The statement on *Industrialization of Building Processes* was published by the National Joint Council on 1 August 1963. Prior to this the Employers' and the Operatives' Federation had been dealing on a rather informal basis with the introduction of new techniques and systems. It was in light of their experience during these discussions that the formal agreement was drafted. The statement first of all recognizes that industrialization of building processes is likely to extend, and that both federations welcome this trend as in the long-term interests of all those in the industry. In the short term, however, redeployment will take place and other fundamental changes will have to be made. It might also be that present working rules, aimed primarily at traditional building processes, may not be very appropriate for a particular industrialized building system.

Nevertheless both federations agree that new processes and techniques must be recognized as building operations. In general they should be performed by building trades operatives at the rates of wages and under the working conditions laid down from time to time by the National Joint Council. However, it is realized that "on the spot" negotiations must take place to cover certain aspects not dealt with by the Working Rules. For instance, the composition of the labour force employed is obviously one important matter which has to be approached with a measure of flexibility. The traditional craft/labour ratio on a normal building site will not be relevant to industrialized systems of building. The agreement therefore aims at the objective of "properly organized teams of building operatives, a broad balance being maintained in the composition of such teams between the numbers of craftsmen and non-craftsmen, as required to meet the demands of the particular operation".

Another very valid point made in the agreement on industrialized systems is that before a new one is introduced, or work started, there should be joint discussions aimed at anticipating points of difficulty. It is because of the realistic approach in the agreement that the rapid industrialization now taking place within the industry has been, in the main, a very peaceful operation.

Incentive Schemes

Following upon the original, and rather briefly worded, 1947 agreement on incentive schemes further reviews have taken place. Because of the widely varying nature of some of the schemes which were operated it was decided that there should be an agreed memorandum on the general principles which should apply. The statement, which is embodied in the National Working Rule book, commences by affirming that the proper use of such schemes should result in better efficiency in output, together with higher earnings for operatives. It then goes on to emphasize that the scheme should be based on standard rates of wages, and operatives should receive extra payment only in respect of extra production based upon stated targets for whatever operation in which they were engaged. These targets should, wherever it is practicable to do so, be agreed between the employer and the accredited representatives of the operatives on-site before any operation is started. The agreement on targets should also be set down in writing for the benefit of the men on-site. A warning is also given that targets should not thereafter be altered unless a material change in the job circumstances arises.

The agreement also faces up to the fact that a high proportion of the disputes within the industry have arisen through difficulties between operatives and employers over the operation of incentive schemes. It asserts that no direct action be taken on the site by either side where a dispute arises but that the matter should be referred to the industry's official machinery.

Early resistance to incentive schemes by the operatives, based upon their fears that standards of safety precautions would decline and that apprentice training would suffer, is also covered by the agreement. Concluding clause 15 emphasizes that:

> In the operation of incentive schemes all concerned must co-operate to ensure
> (a) observance of the Safety, Health and Welfare Regulations
> (b) maintenance of a high standard of workmanship
> (c) adequate training of apprentices
> (d) avoidance of waste of materials
> (e) efficient use of plant.

CHAPTER 10

Solving the Problems

Cost of Bad Industrial Relations

When one considers the complex and fragmented nature of the construction industry, and its highly casual employment of labour, it is surprising that industrial relations are not worse than they are. To some extent traditional custom and practice—in what is perhaps the oldest handcraft industry in the country—may still exert some influence on codes of conduct. There is also the fact that the building worker is the last of the industrial nomads: generally easy going and more tolerant of uncongenial working conditions than industrial workers in the main. Where a "fixed-based" manufacturing worker might feel impelled to strike in support of a grievance against management the building worker —used to casual employment—may simply take his cards and drift off in search of another site where conditions are more tolerable.

If one accepts the theory that the extent to which workers press for better conditions forces management to become more efficient, then this attitude of the operatives may be bad for the industry. Certainly advances in managerial techniques in construction do not appear to have matched the rapid developments in new materials and methods of building. And while other industries are concentrating on bringing managerial aids, such as personnel and labour relations departments, up to a new standard of efficiency the construction industry has yet only set a hesitant foot on this path. Nor is it only the small and medium-sized firm which is at fault. The 1967 *Cameron Report* into the dispute at the Barbican and Horseferry Road construction sites in London[1] clearly shows that even on important prestige jobs, being done by top contractors, there is much room for improvement. While there is no doubt that on both these sites the firms concerned were faced with rather unusual labour troubles, there was still a lot to be desired in the techniques of labour management employed. In fact it was this particular "Achilles heel" which exaggerated the situation and led to ultimate breakdown.

The Horseferry Road job was a government contract worth nearly £5 million and launched in a blaze of publicity because of the high standard of site amenities provided for operatives. Begun in November 1964 it was due for completion by November 1966. But in May of 1967 only half the work was done (see *Cameron Report*, par. 118) and: "With production steadily deteriorating, it appeared that the total wage bill, which had originally been estimated at £700,000 would be about £1,400,000."

Without going into all the features involved in this depressing story it is reasonable to say that the failure was due mainly to a breakdown in industrial relations. Perhaps the most significant fact was that, far from the contracts manager on this extremely important job having the services of a top-class officer to look after industrial relations, he was expected to "double up" and also undertake these duties. The *Cameron Report* (par. 143) comments: "it was unreasonable to expect him to combine these with his main role of Contracts Manager, in particular at a site where there was ample warning that industrial relations were presenting great difficulties."

The mathematics involved for the contractor at the Horseferry Road site is, therefore, how much of the £700,000 additional wage bill necessitated by the breakdown in industrial relations would have been saved by appointing an officer specifically for these duties at a reasonable salary. And almost the same question might be asked of the contractors at the Barbican site who were doing about £5½ million worth of work. Almost the same but not quite: for after trouble had broken out the contractors did finally

[1] *Court of Inquiry Report*, Cmnd. 3396, H.M.S.O., 1967.

appoint a full-time industrial relations officer but (*Cameron Report*, par. 184): "By the time he came into office the situation in the Barbican had reached a critical stage and that appointment had no influence on the course of events as they had developed."

The Barbican job was, of course, bedevilled by (according to the firm) "an unusual number of inconsistent and late instructions from the Architects and other consultants responsible for the contract, which had led to severe difficulties in adhering to the planned programme of work". If this was so, then, in addition to this job showing the poor labour relations which existed, it also appears to have been a classic example of the confusion and division of responsibility for a project which is peculiar to the construction industry.

No doubt there were other factors which influenced events at both the Barbican and Horseferry Road sites and which the contractors would have found it difficult to deal with. It is obvious that when operatives have a built-in resentment against casual employment, it is relatively easy to play on this and influence them towards conflict. It is clear, therefore, that apart from improvements in managerial techniques within individual firms, long-term progress towards better industrial relations depends on the success with which the industry as a whole can overcome these general grievances. In this concluding chapter a few proposals are made with this objective in view.

A Basic Weakness

If there is one basic weakness in construction it is that capitalization of a building firm is far too easy as is the opportunity for almost anyone—qualified or not—to set up in business as a builder. Compared to, say, the few thousands of capital necessary to set up as a sweetshop proprietor, a building firm can be started with almost nothing. The labour-only sub-contractor does not even have to worry about buying materials or plant.

The result is that a large number of people, with no managerial ability or business experience—and perhaps no technical experience either—start operating as "builders". Obviously their capacity for promoting good industrial relations is on a par with their other qualifications! It is sometimes claimed that, while all this may be true, this type of firm is not likely to employ many men and, therefore, their total influence on building is not great. But the matter cannot be shrugged off so easily as that. It simply evades the problem to attack the "one-man-bands" as being the only class likely to contain inefficiency. Even within the medium-size range of builders, and some of the top firms as we have already shown, it is obvious that the level of all-round management expertise which is available is not as high as that employed in other major industries.

A grievance sometimes voiced by the larger firms, which reveals another aspect of the problem, is that they often have to face unfair competition in tendering and this restricts their opportunity to improve conditions and carry out their responsibilities in the way they would wish. The implication here is that certain contractors against whom they are tendering put in low tenders only because they have not allowed realistic overheads for the cost of providing good labour relations; site amenities; safety, health and welfare; guaranteed time and the other provisions of the National Working Rules.

From all of this it is reasonable to conclude that easy capitalization of firms, plus the lack of reasonable uniformity in contracting procedures, leads to a number of serious problems within the construction industry. It is against this background that we should also judge the rapid increase in recent years of labour-only sub-contracting. Unfortunately much of the argument on labour-only has tended to be based on assertions with little factual evidence in support. But without going into all of the detailed arguments there are certain fundamental questions which arise and the answers can be generally agreed on a common knowledge of this method of sub-contracting.

Does anyone, for instance, expect labour-only to directly further improvement in management efficiency? Can it be assumed that labour-only gangs will help with apprentice training—or is it more accurate to say that not one apprentice will be trained by any of them? Will they even pay a levy towards training and thereby the replacement of the craft labour force engaged at present in labour-only gangs? Do these sub-contractors play a part in the organized structure of the industry therefore helping to stabilize it and improve conditions generally? Are, in fact, labour-only gangs sufficiently stable themselves to play such a role?

Most of the answers to the above will surely be in the negative. Yet these are among the most important questions to be put on the significance or otherwise of the contribution any firm makes to improving the industry in which it works and from which it draws its income. Taking the most objective view possible it seems reasonable to conclude that the growth of labour-only is not likely to lead to greater progress and well-being within the construction industry. These sub-contractors are, perhaps, the supreme example of how "firms" without management expertise or financial backing can mushroom in the construction industry.

Again the argument may be raised that most of these sub-contractors are in a small way of business and have little influence on the industry generally. But when one considers the total labour force employed by them the picture takes on a new significance. Figures on this were produced by the Construction Industry Training Board in 1965 as a result of a survey relating to main contractors employing labour-only gangs. The Board finally compiled a list of over 45,000 labour-only firms and then circularized them about their responsibility for paying the industrial training levy.

The result? Fifteen thousand of these circulars were returned by the G.P.O. dead letter office because the firms could not be traced and another 16,000 just did not reply. Seven thousand who did reply claimed they were not liable to pay training levy as they were either self-employed or in partnership with self-employed persons. Another 7,000 forms were returned by firms who disclaimed responsibility on the grounds that their total annual wage bill was less than the amount required for paying the levy. The final result was that out of the 45,000 firms written to only 647 conceded any liability to pay for industrial training.

These figures, apart from revealing that only about 1·4 per cent of labour-only sub-contractors admitted responsibility for contributing to training which is essential for the future of the industry, also show the extent to which labour-only has developed. All of the "firms" circularized were supposed to be employing labour. If these gangs averaged around four to six people each, and one adds to this the number of self-employed persons doing labour-only work, then the grand total may be around a quarter of a million men.

When one adds this figure to the number of operatives employed by small builders, and bona fide sub-contractors, it becomes clear that the influence of these firms is upon a considerable part of construction's total labour force. The weaknesses which exist in many of them are therefore of real importance for the industry. This is not to say, however, that there is a general case against small-scale operations in building. Client demand is so varied and wide-ranging that small firms can effectively satisfy a part of it and, in fact, can probably do so better than the larger contractors who are geared up to do a different category of work. What is essential is that, at whatever level a firm operates, it should be competent in a technical and managerial sense, and have a reasonable degree of financial stability. But in what way does one effectively apply these qualifications to builders? How can it be ensured that the "bad" firms do not gradually drive down standards in general? The most satisfactory answer seems to be the establishment of a national register of firms in the construction industry.

National Register of Builders

Before being able to undertake building work a firm would have to apply and be accepted on this register, and the registration board's most important duty would be to devise qualifications to be applied to applicants. Mr. John G. Snelling, FIOB (a leading figure in the NFBTE), has considered this particular point and consequently listed a number of qualifications which he thinks such a registration board should require applicants to fulfil. He believes the a builder should be able to assure the board that:

1. He has adequate financial reserves or backing to cover his first three months' trading.
2. He has some qualification: this to be not less than the Higher National Certificate. Membership of the Institute obviously would be prima facie evidence of standard.
3. He has been engaged in the building industry for at least 10 years. This would assume that he had completed a 5-year apprenticeship and a 5-year probationary period with a builder or in his chosen trade.
4. He has acquired some administrative and organising ability either through previous employment or by an examination after a course on building management, or something similar.[2]

Qualifications such as these, however they might subsequently be refined, would certainly ensure that a registered builder was basically capable of satisfying industrial requirements in addition to providing a reasonable guarantee for his clients. Certain employers, while agreeing that these twin objectives are desirable, emphasize that they would not approve a government-controlled national register as the way to achieve them.

There is no reason why, however, such a registration board should not be set up as an independent body in the same way that some professional institutes were created. Professor Norman Sidwell, of Heriot-Watt University and a leading spokesman on the subject of registration, has written about the compulsory registration scheme which applies in Western Australia and is administered by a five-member Registration Board. Established under the 1939 Builders Registration Act the Board comprises two architects, two builders and one member representing building operatives. The basic functions of the Board are to determine the course of training and level of experience necessary for registration, to keep a register of builders admitted, to issue or cancel certificates of registration and to take proceedings for offences against the Act, and generally to administer its provisions.

[2] From his article in the June 1967 issue of *Building Technology and Management*.

Professor Sidwell adds that, while no one can accuse Australians of being "regulation minded", the register has existed for nearly 30 years and has won general approval for its value in maintaining good standards among firms in construction. Some British builders, however, still questioning the need for such a register in this country claim that the National House Builders Registration Council at present fills such a role and especially since it has been officially backed by the Minister of Housing and Local Government. The NHBRC, however, does not serve as a completely satisfactory alternative to a national register of builders for two major reasons. First it has a narrower concept in that it is basically an insurance scheme, aimed at protecting purchasers, whereas the builders' registration board would have much broader responsibility in judging a firm's all-round competence. Secondly, the NHBRC scheme relates only to the building of new houses—a minority of total construction output—but a national register of firms would apply to all those undertaking work in the industry.

Another point of view which has emerged recently is that events are now proceeding in such a way that a national register will not be required. It is claimed that since the report from the Banwell Committee, on the Placing and Management of Contracts, many building clients and especially public authorities are increasingly adopting selective tendering. As this obviously requires prior selection of firms invited to tender, so local builders' registration lists are effectively coming into existence and making a national register superfluous. But surely it cannot make for satisfactory registration, or uniform standards of qualifications, if 1000 local authorities apply their differing yardsticks to builders before placing them on their "registers". In any event local authorities could only normally adjudicate on firms tendering within their immediate localities. What happens when a contractor 200 miles away wishes to tender? Does a local authority refuse because he is not on their list; which really means that all outside contractors would eventually be excluded and work confined to local firms? Or should it make a cross-check with another local authority to find out the standing of the contractor in question?

Any of the procedures would be very unsatisfactory and therefore only a national register could guarantee general standards of competence being applied, while giving clients a central point of reference. When one examines the Banwell Report, and what is said about the desirability of more efficiency and selectivity in tendering, it becomes increasingly clear that the implementation of Banwell rests on the provision of some central reference to the competence of construction firms in general: not only for the clients' benefit, but also for the guidance of the professions and those having to deal with contractors. Therefore, irrespective of possible uneasiness about the proposal or the difficulties which may have to be surmounted, the register is a matter which must be considered as a necessary step to the future well-being of the industry and the basis for improving all round efficiency. Implementation of such a register will also end the paradoxical situation where the building professions are generally subject to qualifications and control, but not the firms which erect the structures designed and planned by them.

Register of Operatives

Registration of firms should also help to raise general standards in the industry and, in consequence, lead to more efficient site-work, thereby improving conditions for the operatives. In this way better industrial relations will gradually evolve. To a certain degree there will also be less casual employment because efficient management should not only mean a decrease in bankruptcies, and other industrial failings, but lead to improved methods for winter building and during inclement weather generally. This is not to say, however, that construction will manage to bring down casualization to the level which applies in other industries.

For even if ultimately quite a large amount of prefabrication takes place in factories the construction product will always have to be assembled on the actual site chosen by the client. There may be anything around one million sites in operation at any one time. And contractors will be constantly transferring from site to site as one job finishes and another opens up. The new contract may be many miles away and the employer will find a large number of his men unwilling to travel: he must therefore face the necessity of building up a fresh labour force for his new job. Or there may be no new job available when he has finished the current one, and his labour force will have to be dispersed in any event. In fact his contracts will usually come irregularly and he will be justified in claiming that, if his resources are used so casually and sporadically, he is hardly able to offer long-term guarantees to his workmen.

All this is the unavoidable consequence of a very large number of firms competing for contracts at all levels. The mass of operatives in such an industry are therefore bound to be excluded from those benefits for which qualification is the length of service with an individual employer. This fundamental truth was recognized by the special collective provisions made for giving holidays with pay. And it would seem that progress towards further improvement in conditions must lie in recognizing that, in an industry where casual employment is endemic, extension of benefits for operatives must be on a collective rather than individual firm basis. This, in turn, implies some form of central registration for operatives.

One advantage is that it would be relatively easy to implement such an operatives' registration board because basic facilities already exist within the offices of the Holidays With Pay Scheme. In effect it does have a register which, until recently, only existed for the purpose of holidays with pay. Then the sickness and accident benefit, introduced into the National Working Rules, was grafted onto the Holidays With Pay Scheme. This was a good example of the way in which the Holidays With Pay Scheme could be used to introduce a valuable benefit for operatives with almost no extra administrative costs being incurred. Yet the scheme's administration is still being under-exploited and the time is now opportune for reconsidering its general role. Instead of being used primarily for administration of holidays it could be turned into a registration board for operatives. The length of time an operative was registered with the board would be the qualification upon which fringe benefits would be given to him—holidays with pay still being administered on much the same basis as at present. Sickness and accident benefits have now been introduced: there are a number of others which could be speedily implemented if the registration board was implemented.

Pensions and Death Benefit

First of all there is the question of a pension for construction operatives. In Southern Ireland a scheme already exists, based on annual stamp cards being issued whereon a pension stamp is affixed by employers for each operative. At the end of each year the number of stamps on the annual card is transferred to a master card for the operative and his record is then continuous and kept up to date.

Apart from the value of such a scheme to the operatives, the industry would also clearly benefit. It is because construction workers have so few amenities, and very little binding them to the industry, that they are able to opt out of it without loss. But if a man was building up his pension with every week of service he would think very seriously before he left the industry and thereby destroyed those entitlements.

Another benefit which is overdue in construction is a death by accident benefit. The industry is one of the most dangerous in Britain. Accidents are rising almost every year and, at present, an average of between 250 and 270 men are killed every year. Due to the casual nature of the industry most operatives are unable to save reasonable sums of money to help their dependants in these distressing circumstances, and a financial burden is added to grief. If every operative registered on the board were entitled to the payment of £100 death by accident benefit to his next of kin this would be something that would bring more ease of mind to those working in construction. At the present rate of deaths such a benefit would only mean a total annual payment of £27,000 and this would hardly be considered a very large sum when compared with the total number of men in the industry, or the beneficial results of having such a scheme. In addition to the payment of this benefit any accrued pension entitlements would also go to the next of kin. The provision of pensions and a death benefit would therefore be a valuable extension to those already existing.

Redundancy Payments

When the 1963 Redundancy Payments Act was brought in the construction unions said that it would have little affect on building operatives. For, under the Act, a worker has to be employed by a firm for not less than 2 years continuously before being entitled to any payment. As it has been estimated that only around 15–25 per cent of men in construction are employed on a reasonably permanent basis it is clear that the great majority would not qualify for benefit, claimed the unions. Yet under the terms of the Act there has to be a contribution of $10d.$ per week paid to the central redundancy fund for each operative employed: the construction industry is therefore making contributions to the fund but not drawing in proportion upon it due to the excessively casual nature of employment.

This argument by the unions brings into question the entire meaning of the term "redundancy". If it fits the common conception that it relates to an employee who, after long service in an industry, is discharged with little immediate prospect of further employment then obviously the construction operative does not fit into this picture. His casual employment is a feature of the industry and any unemployment is looked upon as generally transitional between jobs.

But if redundancy payments are, in effect, "discharge payments" irrespective of whether or not an employee has a job to go to the following week (and some recent decisions appear to indicate this) then the unions may be right in claiming that the building operative suffers a disadvantage. At the same time if any measures were taken to overcome this, so that building operatives could also get discharge payments, then the central redundancy fund would probably be bankrupted in view of the high labour turn-over in the industry!

It would therefore seem that there is a valid case for allowing construction to set up its own redundancy scheme in view of the industry's special circumstances. This could be administered through the operatives national register already envisaged. The Minister of Labour could give discretion to the registration board to decide its own definition of redundancy and the scale of pay-ments to meet it—always accepting that the Minister must have overriding powers. The *per capita* payment of 10*d*. per week per operative, made to the central redundancy fund at present, could then be transferred to the registration board (the total perhaps amounting to £2½ million per year) which could use it to supple-ment the amounts to be given to the operative by his employer.

Inclement Weather and Guaranteed Time

Apart from the effects of total redundancy there is the fact that inclement weather makes for "sporadic redundancy" and loss of earnings. This has been a source of grievance to operatives for many years and the National Working Rules have been amended frequently in an attempt to set down reasonable guaran-tees. Of course there is the valid theory that the best way to cut inclement weather loss is to take steps to ensure that work can be carried out during bad weather, and especially in the winter. For, in this season, not only does bad weather intervene but also much production is lost due to hours of darkness coming in earlier and no provision being made for adequate artificial lighting. This certainly seems to be the most satisfactory solution but, however, it has to be assumed that there will be times when a shut-down of operations takes place which finally results in men being discharged to the local employment exchange.

The most severe winter in past years was that in 1963. In addition to operatives not being able to earn it was calculated that around £100 million worth of output was also lost. What was incalculable was the time and money expended due to the disintegration of labour forces which had to be re-formed when jobs finally commenced activities again. Nor was the general atmosphere of uncertainty and dismissal to the dole queue beneficial to future industrial relations. Yet it was an event that need not have taken place, given certain provisions in the National Working Rules and co-operation from the Government. There is no sense in discharging men to the employment exchange at a time when, due to a general shut-down in the industry, there is no employment to exchange (of course some of the operatives take the opportunity of employment outside construction and are probably lost to the industry for good). Therefore, if unemployment benefit is their only prospect surely a system could be devised where an equivalent sum could be drawn without men having to officially sever their employment?

How would such a scheme work? At present employers pay for intermittent lost time, during a shower of rain or a few hours of frost, and they are also committed to one week's full guarantee of 36 hours' pay in the event of really hard weather. Thereafter they can sack their men and the State must pay unemployment benefit to keep them and their families until the weather improves sufficiently to allow building operations to recommence.

If a national register of operatives existed it is proposed that the employer should be able, after meeting his inclement weather payment as laid down under National Working Rules, to draw stand-by pay for his men from the registration board for any additional time in which they are unable to work due to bad weather. Any such operatives would have to be on the register, of course, and the employer would also have to supply proof that he had met his commitment to them under the National Working Rule and that work was still not able to proceed for a further period. The basic stand-by pay would be that which the men would have received from the Ministry of Labour exchanges, and that Ministry could arrange for the transfer of the appropriate amounts to the operatives registration board: the Ministry loses nothing as it would have to pay out the money in any case.

In addition to this basic amount the inclement-weather fund could be built up by weekly stamp instalments out of which a supplementary payment could be made. The total value of such a scheme to the operative would be very great because, as he would no longer have to officially sever his employment, his social security and other stamp credits would continue, thus maintaining full entitlements to fringe benefits in general. The employer and the industry as a whole would also derive value from the scheme because labour forces would be kept intact, together with the know-how built up on a particular job, and they would be ready to resume operations as soon as it was possible. It is justifiably claimed that, after a bad weather shut-down in the industry, it is often months before full production is regained again. By being able to keep experienced labour forces together this period of optimum resumption of work would surely be much less.

Obviously introduction of such a scheme would mean recognizing the special circumstances of the construction industry. It is time, however, to realize that legislation cannot be applied equally to all industries with resultant equality for all. Justice depends upon unique circumstances being adequately met. And if the state does make special efforts to help attain the ends stated, surely—in a period where the building product is of great social importance—it also benefits from the increased industrial efficiency which arises as a consequence.

It is also clear that it is only through the employer and union organizations taking a more radical view of what might be done that solutions to construction's most persistent problems will be found. A register for employers and one for the operatives, it is proposed, will help achieve the objectives desired by both sides. By striving towards greater order in construction through these means they will also be directly bringing about changes which will result in an atmosphere conducive to improved industrial relations.

LIST OF OPERATIONS INCLUDED WITHIN THE SCOPE OF THE CONSTRUCTION INDUSTRY

Range of Operations Involved in Construction[1]

1. All operations in the construction, alteration, repair, maintenance, re-pointing, re-decoration, external cleaning or demolition of a building (which includes any structure or erection).

2. All operations in the construction or demolition of a railway line, siding or monorail.

3. The construction, structural alteration, repair or demolition of the following:

Adit
Aerodrome
Airport
Aqueduct
Bore-hole
Bridge
Cable trench or
    duct
Canal or inland
    navigation
Carbonizing plant
Chimney
Coast protection
    work
Cooling tower or
    pond

Defence installation
Dock
Electric line or any
    structure designed
    for its support
Filter bed
Furnace
Gas making plant
Harbour
Hydro-electric
    station
Nuclear or thermal
    power station
Oil refinery
Pier
Pipeline

Quay
Reservoir
River or drainage
    work
Road
Sewer
Sewage works
Tunnel
Viaduct
Waterworks
Well, other than an
    oil well
Wharf

[1] The list of operations is that issued as a guide by the Construction Industry Training Board.

4. The preparation of a site or laying down of a foundation or sub-structure in connection with any of the activities mentioned at 1, 2 or 3 above, or with the erection of structural metalwork.

5. The construction of a swimming pool or other bathing place.

The construction of a playing field or ground for sporting or recreational purpose.

The laying out of a cemetery.

6. The provision or continued provision for any building or construction or work above mentioned of water, gas, electricity, lighting, heating or ventilation when these operations are undertaken in, upon, above or under

the building or its close, curtilage or precincts or any construction, work or site mentioned above.

7. The erection or dismantling of
Fencing
Hoarding
Scaffolding

8. The preparation of stone for building purposes.

9. All operations in the manufacture of
Bank, church, laboratory or other joinery.

Doors
Window frames
Built-in storage units } constructed wholly or mainly from wood
Stairs
Curtain walling

A prefabricated building or section of a building (not being constructed wholly or mainly from metal or from a combination of metal and plastic material).

10. The construction of shop, office or similar fittings on the premises on which they are to be installed.

11. The erection or dismantling of exhibition stands.

12. The hiring out of contractors' plant or scaffolding.

13. Any of the following when carried out in conjunction with any of the foregoing activities:

Research
Development
Design or drawing
Operations in connection with:
  Sale
  Packing
  Warehousing
  Distribution
  Transport
Work done at an:
  Office
  Laboratory
  Store
  Warehouse or similar place
  Garage

14. Any other activity of industry or commerce carried out at or from an establishment engaged mainly in one or more of the foregoing activities.

APPENDIX 2

CONSTITUTION, RULES AND REGULATIONS OF THE NATIONAL JOINT COUNCIL FOR THE BUILDING INDUSTRY

Constitution, Rules and Regulations

As adopted by the Council and the Adherent Bodies, 4th November, 1963.

MEMORANDUM OF AGREEMENT

MEMORANDUM OF AGREEMENT *between the Employers' and Operatives' National Federations and Associations connected with the Building Trades who are signatories to this Agreement.*

Clause 1. It is agreed that the rates of Wages of Workmen employed in the Building Industry, the Hours of Labour, and such other matters as are mentioned in the Rules, Regulations and Working Rules hereunder, except as hereinafter expressly provided in Rule 12 and Regulation 11, shall be determined on a National basis.

Clause 2. Pursuant to the terms of Clause 1 hereof, the Parties hereto (namely, the Bodies which have given their adhesion hereto by the signatures of their President and Secretary) jointly and severally declare that unless and until their adherence to this Agreement is terminated in the manner hereinafter provided they will not permit, endorse, sanction or otherwise condone any claim or agreement to vary (except as aforesaid) any of the matters mentioned in the Rules, Regulations and Working Rules hereunder, and having for its object the determination of any of those matters on any other than a National basis, and will respectively use all means in their power to prevent or nullify any such claim or agreement.

Clause 3. It is further agreed that, in order to carry out this Agreement according to its true intent and meaning, a National Joint Council shall be appointed and the following Rules, Regulations and Working Rules, together with such Variation Amendments as have been sanctioned, adopted and/or recorded by the Council and with such Constitutional and Variation Amendments as may be made by the prescribed procedure, shall be observed during the currency of the Agreement.

Clause 4. (*a*) The Council shall consist of not more than forty Members, half of whom shall be Employers' Representatives and half Operatives' Representatives apportioned among and appointed annually by the parties affiliated to the Council in such manner as the respective sides shall from time to time agree, to take office at each Annual Meeting.

(*b*) All Members of the Council shall retire annually, but shall be eligible for re-appointment. The annual appointment of the Members of the Council shall be notified to the Clerk prior to the Annual Meeting.

(*c*) Any casual vacancy occurring during the year shall be filled by the body which appointed the Member whose place has become vacant.

Clause 5. The duties of the Council shall be:

(*a*) To deal, in accordance with the Rules and Regulations hereinafter provided, with the following matters:

    (i) Rates of Wages.

    (ii) Working Hours.

    (iii) Extra Payments.

    (iv) Overtime.

    (v) Night Gangs.

    (vi) Travelling and Lodging Allowances.

    (vii) Guaranteed Payments in relation to Time Lost.

    (viii) Termination of Employment.

    (ix) Apprenticeship.

    (x) Holiday Payments.

    (xi) Safety, Health and Welfare Conditions.

(*b*) To adjust all differences or disputes that may from time to time arise and be referred to the Council by either Employers or Operatives with a view to an amicable settlement of the same without resort to strikes or lock-outs.

(*c*) To provide for such references to the constituent bodies as may be necessary in the case of a decision or decisions involving a Constitutional Amendment (under Rule 10) or any other question which the Council wishes to refer to the members of the constituent bodies for approval or otherwise.

(*d*) To give binding decisions in cases involving Variation Amendments (under Rule 12 or the Working Rules), and

(*e*) To make such provisions as may appear necessary from time to time for the better carrying out of this Agreement and generally to do all things necessary to the furtherance or attainment of the foregoing objects or any of them.

Clause 6. In carrying out these duties the Council shall delegate such powers as are appropriate under the Rules and Regulations hereinafter set out, to:—

(i) *Regional Joint Committees*, which shall be set up in accordance with Regulation 8, to deal with the initiation of Variation Amendments (under Rule 12) and with differences or disputes under Rule 9, in respect of the "Region" which they are authorised to administer by the National Joint Council.

(ii) *Area Joint Committees,* in such cases where such are appointed by Regional Joint Committees to deal with their respective "Areas" in the manner set out in Regulation 10. Such Committees may possess powers, if so arranged by the Regional Joint Committees, of initiating and dealing with Variation Amendments.

(iii) *Local Joint Committees* which shall have powers in connection with Overtime (Working Rule 4A): the fixing of agreed "free area" boundaries (Working Rule 6A), together with the general duty of regulating the operation of the Working Rules (within the limits defined in those Rules) in their respective "Districts".

It shall also be the duty of the Local Joint Committee to define the boundaries of the territory with which they deal, subject always (in cases of disagreement of alleged encroachment upon other districts) to overriding powers hereby reserved to the appropriate Regional Joint Committee or National Standing Committees.

Clause 7. For the purpose of this Agreement the following definitions shall apply:

A District is the territory with which a Local Joint Committee deals and the boundaries of which have been defined as required by clause 6 (iii) above.

An Area is a large District, or group of Districts, specified by a Regional Joint Committee as being under the control of an Area Joint Committee to which may be delegated (under Regulation 10) powers and duties consistent with those relating to Regional Joint Committees.

A Region is a large Area, or group of Areas and/or Districts, united under a Regional Joint Committee as may be arranged by the National Joint Council.

Clause 8. The Parties hereto agree that their adherence to the Council shall be terminated only in accordance with the provision of Rule 16.

RULES

1. (*a*) The Council shall meet regularly in February (not later than the 14th day thereof); in July; and in October.

The dates for the next three successive regular meetings of the Council shall be fixed in advance at the Annual Meeting.

The February meeting of the Council shall be known as the "Annual Meeting".

Other meetings of the Council shall be held at such other times as the Council, or the Chairman acting on its behalf, may appoint.

(*b*) A Special Meeting shall be held upon a requisition signed by any ten Members of the Council. Such requisition must state the business for which the meeting is to be held.

(*c*) Fourteen days' notice shall be given of an Annual Meeting, and seven days' notice of any other meeting of the Council. Agenda papers and all relevant documents shall be circulated to Members of the Council at least seven days prior to the date of the convened meeting.

2. (*a*) The Officers of the Council, who shall be *ex-officio* Members of all Standing Committees of the Council, shall consist of a Chairman and Vice-Chairman, elected from among the Members of the Council, together with two Honorary Joint Secretaries, one appointed each by the Employers' and Operatives' sides of the Council respectively.

(*b*) The Standing Committees of the Council shall include:—

(i) A Procedure Committee.

(ii) A General Purposes Committee.

   (iii) A Conciliation Panel.
   (iv) An Apprentices' Conditions Committee.
   (v) A National Joint Apprenticeship Board.
   (vi) An Appeal Committee (Apprentice Deeds Disputes).
   (vii) A Factories and Shops Committee.
   (viii) An Industrial Safety, Health and Welfare Committee.

The constitution, personnel, duties and powers of the Standing Committees shall be such as may be determined from time to time by the Council. Minutes of the Meetings of Standing Committees shall be mutually agreed by the Joint Secretaries and the Chairman of the appropriate Committee.

(c) A Clerk (who will also be the Treasurer) shall be appointed by the Council upon such terms as the Council may determine and, under the direction of the Joint Secretaries, he shall act as Clerk and Treasurer to the Council and its various Committees; shall summon meetings; keep Minutes; conduct correspondence; receive and pay to the Council's Bankers all subscriptions and other money received on behalf of the Council; keep proper accounts; prepare and, where necessary, issue reports and discharge all duties customarily undertaken by a Secretary and Treasurer. He shall render to the Council yearly at the Annual Meeting of the Council an account of all sums received and paid on behalf of the Council, and shall present at such Annual Meeting an audited statement of accounts. *Clerk to Council.*

(d) The accounts shall be audited by a Chartered Accountant, appointed by the Annual Meeting. *Auditors.*

3. (a) The expenses incurred by the Council shall be borne as to one-half by the bodies represented *Council's Expenses.*

on the Employers' side and as to one-half by those represented on the Operatives' side, and each side shall apportion the share it has to bear among the constituent bodies thereof as may be agreed among them from time to time.

Council
Members'
Expenses.

(b) The expenses of Members of the Council attending meetings of the Council, meetings of Committees thereof, and such other meetings as the Council shall direct, shall be met from the funds of the Council. The expenses of other representatives convened to such meetings may also be met where the Council so directs.

Council's
Estimates.

(c) An estimate of the probable expenses of the Council for the ensuing year shall be presented by the Clerk at the Annual Meeting thereof, and if approved by the Council shall become due and payable by the respective constituent bodies in accordance with their respective shares apportioned as aforesaid.

Signature of
Cheques.

(d) All cheques for withdrawal of money from the Council's Bankers on behalf of the Council shall be signed by the Clerk to the Council and countersigned by the Joint Secretaries.

Notifications,
Minutes
and Press
Statements.

4. After each meeting of the Council the Clerk shall give notice of the findings to all concerned as early as possible, and in any case within fourteen days, and shall prepare and cause the Minutes thereof to be printed and issued as soon as possible thereafter. The Minutes shall be mutually agreed by the Joint Secretaries and the Chairman before issue.

At the close of each meeting of the Council, and as may be instructed by the Council, the Joint Secretaries may prepare and issue to the Press an agreed statement of the outcome of the meeting.

5. A majority of the Members of the Council on ᵗch side shall constitute a quorum at any meeting ᵗ the Council.

6. Ordinarily voting shall be by show of hands ᵗt shall be by ballot upon request of either side. ᵗny decision to be binding must be carried by a ᵗajority of votes on each side of those present and ᵗting. The Chairman shall have one vote only as a ᵗember of the Council.

7. Should either side desire to retire for private ᵗnsultation during any sitting of the Council it ᵗall be allowed to do so.

8. Should any Member of the Council be unable ᵗ attend any meeting of the Council, a substitute ᵗly appointed by the body he represents, may attend ᵗ his place upon due notice in writing being given ᵗ the Clerk.

9. (*a*) The Council (either directly or through its ᵗpropriate Standing Committee) shall deal with ᵗ differences or disputes referred to it under its ᵗnstitution and Rules, whether concerned with the ᵗterpretation of its own decisions or otherwise.

(*b*) Any difference or dispute that may arise in ᵗy locality involving or likely to involve members ᵗ any party affiliated to the National Joint Council ᵗr the Building Industry shall be dealt with in ᵗcordance with the procedure set out in the National ᵗnergency Disputes Agreement* (commonly refer- ᵗd to as "Green Book Procedure") for the purpose ᵗ:

(i) *Preventing any cessation of work or of securing a resumption of work in cases where cessation has taken place;*

* See Appendix 4.

(ii) *Referring the difference or dispute in th* *prescribed manner to the appropriate machine* *for settlement thereof; or*

(iii) *Arranging, if the difference or dispute is n* *so referable, that it be dealt with by the appropria* *Joint Emergency Disputes Commission, whi* *may give such directions and make such repor* *and recommendations to the respective nation* *executives as are provided for in the Nation* *Emergency Disputes Agreement.*

(c) A difference or dispute referred, under sectio (b) (ii) above, to the National Joint Council machi ery, shall be dealt with by a Regional Standi Conciliation Panel appointed under Regulatio 9, who shall hear, and if possible determine, tl case as soon as possible, and in any case with 21 days. The decision of such Regional Conciliatio Panel shall be final and binding (for the territory t which it applies) unless notice of appeal is given t one or other of the disputants to the Clerk of tl National Joint Council within 7 days of the da thereof. Such decisions shall not constitute prec dents. It shall be competent for the Chairman the Standing Conciliation Panel in consultation wil the Joint Secretaries, upon being satisfied that a appellent party through circumstances outwith the control has been unable to comply with the 7-da rule referred to above, to accept an appeal fc national hearing after the date prescribed. Tl decision of the officers shall be final in all such case

In the event of a Regional Conciliation Pan failing to reach a decision upon an issue so referre they may refer the matter to the National Joi Council but, in the absence of such reference, tl parties concerned shall have the right of appeal t

ιe National Joint Council. Such an appeal or
ference having been made, the Regional Joint
ιcretaries concerned shall forward within 7 days
ιereof to the Clerk of the National Joint Council
ιe Minutes and all relevant documents relating
ι the matter, for reference to, and hearing and
ιtermination by, the National Conciliation Panel
˚ that body. The appeal or reference shall be dealt
ιth as soon as possible by the National Concilia-
ɔn Panel of the National Joint Council, whose
ιcision shall be final and binding. The proceedings
˚ such Panel shall duly be reported to the National
ιint Council at its next meeting and be received
ιd entered upon its Minutes.

(*d*) The procedure at hearings of Conciliation
ιses shall conform to that laid down in the Regula-
ɔns of the Council. Where interpretation of the
ιational Joint Council Agreement or elucidation of
ιational Joint Council decisions, appears advisable,
ιe National Conciliation Panel may seek advice
˚ guidance through the Procedure Committee of
ιe Council.

(*e*) In the event of the Conciliation Panel of the
ιational Joint Council failing to reach a decision
ι regard to any case, it shall report accordingly to
ιe next meeting of the National Joint Council,
ιgether with Minutes of the proceedings in regard
ι the case in question and all relevant documents
ιlating thereto. Whereupon, it shall be the duty
˚ the National Joint Council, at such meeting, to
ιnsider the said Minutes and documents for the
ιrpose of ascertaining:

(i) Whether it can suggest a solution of the
matter and refer it back to the Conciliation Panel

for the suggestion to be considered and a decisi〈
arrived at: or

(ii) Whether it shall proceed to deal with t〉
matter in accordance with the provisions
Rule 13 hereof.

In any event the parties concerned in the differen〉
or dispute shall be duly informed of the result
such consideration by the Council.

Constitutional Amendments: Definition of

10. (*a*) A "Constitutional Amendment" shall mea〉
one which proposes to alter the essence of th〉
Constitution or any Agreement essential theret〉
as distinct from a "Variation Amendment" 〈
defined in Rule 12.

How Proposed.

(*b*) A Constitutional Amendment may be propos〈
at the Annual Meeting or at the July or Octob〈
Ordinary meetings. Any party to this Agreeme〉
desiring to propose a Constitutional Amendme〉
must give to the Clerk and to the Joint Secretari〈
written notice of such intention eight weeks pri〈
to the date fixed for the Annual, July or Octob〈
meeting as the case may be. The notice must speci〉
precisely the nature of the proposed Amendmen〉

Upon receipt of such notice the Clerk shall cau〉
the proposal to be circulated to all other Parti〈
hereto, who shall be allowed 14 days within whi〈
to enter Constitutional Amendment Notices then
selves. Where desired the Procedure Committ〈
may be consulted as to the regularity or otherwi〉
of any proposal intended for submission as a Const
tutional Amendment notice, prior to its submissio〉

Consideration by Council.

(*c*) Due notice having been given in accordan〈
with the requirements of (*b*) above, the propos〉
shall be presented to the Council for consideratic
at its next regular meeting.

(*d*) A Constitutional Amendment proposed to be made under a decision of the Council shall be subject to ratification and shall be submitted by the Council accordingly to the Adherent Bodies for such ratification before taking effect.

Ratification.

(*e*) Before submitting such decision of the Council for ratification, the Council shall agree upon the terms of reference to the Adherent Bodies, which shall be allowed four weeks from the date of the decision within which to express their opinion for or against. Where in the exercise of its constitutional powers the Council receives a Constitutional Amendment notice as an agreed joint submission from the Executives of the Adherent Bodies, it shall be permissible for prior ratification to be declared and accepted at the meeting.

Ratification: Terms of Reference and Allotted Time.

(*f*) The opinions of the Parties shall be reported to the Procedure Committee of the Council. The value to be attached to the vote of each Party hereto is to be proportional to its share of representation on the Council. A decision in favour of ratification by a majority of the Employers, Parties hereto, and a decision in favour of ratification by a majority of the Operatives, Parties hereto, shall carry ratification. Thereupon, the Procedure Committee shall be instructed to promulgate the decision and publish the date from which it shall operate. Such a decision shall become binding upon the Industry accordingly.

Ratification. How Carried.

(*g*) Should there be failure to ratify, the Council shall meet as soon as practicable thereafter to consider what further steps, if any, it can take in the matter.

Failure to Ratify.

(*h*) Once a Constitutional Amendment has, after due notice, been proposed to the Annual Meeting of the Council or to a July or October Ordinary

Limitation on Re-introduction of Proposals or Submission of New Proposals.

Meeting, whatever the outcome of the proposal
may be and whether a decision of the Council on
the proposal has or has not been ratified, no further
proposal affecting the same provision of the Council's
Agreements shall be considered by the Council
earlier than the Annual Meeting, July meeting or
October meeting held one year after the meeting
when the original proposal was made.

Annual Wage Review Sliding Scale.

Grade A Rates.

11. (*a*) At each Annual Meeting the Council shall
ascertain from the figures published by the Ministry
of Labour in each of the antecedent 12 months
(January to December) the Average Retail Prices
Index figure* for that antecedent period. A Grade A
standard rate for craftsmen of 5/8½d. per hour is
taken to correspond to a Retail Price Index-range of
100 and up to but not including 102 points. Each
two-point interval, up or down, from that index-
range shall correspond to ½d. per hour, up or down,
in the Grade A standard rate.

For example:

98 and up to but not including 100—½d. lower
102   ,,   ,,   ,,   104—½d. higher

and so on, with ½d. difference at each 2-point interval,
up or down, in the index-range.

Having ascertained the average index figure as
above, the Council shall make a decision adjusting
the current Grade A standard rate accordingly.
The decision shall apply equally to all current standard rates from which Differential Rates of wages
are derived (as prescribed under Rule 12 (*b*)).

* NOTE: The Retail Prices Index Figures referred to in this
Rule are based on the January 1956 Index. The figures published by the Ministry of Labour under the Revised Index
based on price levels at January 1962 = 100, are converted
to the 1956 Index by applying the following formula: 1962
Index figures × 1.175 = 1956 Index figures.

(*b*) The corresponding current labourers' rate shall be 9½d. per hour below the current standard rate as decided by the Council in accordance with Paragraph (*a*) of this rule.

(*c*) Wage adjustments made under this Rule shall take effect at the beginning of the first pay-week of the month immediately following the date of review.

(*d*) The special current standard rate for London shall be the current standard "A" grade rate for the time being in operation, plus 1½d. per hour. The corresponding labourers' rate for London shall be 9½d. per hour below the special current standard rate.

London Rates.

(*e*) The special current standard rate for the Liverpool District (as constitutionally defined) shall be the current standard "A" grade rate for the time being in operation, plus 1½d. per hour. The corresponding labourers' rate shall be 9½d. per hour below the special current standard rate.

Liverpool Rates.

12. A Variation Amendment means one which does not alter the essence of this Constitution or any agreement essential thereto, as distinct from a Constitutional Amendment as defined in Rule 10 (*a*).

Variation Amendments. Definition of.

The following provisions shall govern "Variation Amendments".

(*a*) Upon any question of variation arising under this Rule—whether initiated Regionally for Regional or Area application or by a proposal of a National Standing Committee for National application—decisions of the Council shall be final and binding.

Council Decisions are Final.

(*b*) A "Differential Rate of Wages" is one which applies to a section of the Industry in a defined

Differential Margins.

district but which differs, by a special hourly margin (termed "the differential margin"):

(A) In the case of craftsmen, from the current standard rate applicable to the district:

(B) In the case of labourers, from the labourers' rate corresponding to the current standard rate applicable to the district.

Differential margins recognised by the Council by reason of their having existed at the time of the National Joint Council's inception (September 22nd, 1926) were not vitiated by the fixing of the foregoing standard rates, but it shall be competent for any Party or Parties to this Agreement in any Region dealing with Variation Amendments as a Regional unit, or otherwise in any Area:

(i) Desiring to alter or remove a differential margin already recognised as applying to a section of the Industry in a district within that Region or Area; or

(ii) Desiring to apply a differential margin to any section of the industry in a district within that Region or Area;

to initiate an application for an appropriate Variation Amendment to be dealt with in the manner, and according to the provisions, prescribed in the Rules and Regulations herein.

Order of Dealing with. (c) Questions of differential margins shall be dealt with by the Council on their merits prior to dealing with any question as to whether any adjustment is required under Rule 11 (a) hereof.

National Working Rules. Variations of. (d) Where a Regional or Area Joint Committee receives due notice for the initiation of a variation from or under Rules 2 to 6 inclusive of the National Working Rules so far as that Region or Area is concerned, it shall be competent for such a variation of the said Rules (or any of them) to be proposed, to meet Regional or Area circumstances, in the manner provided by the Rules and Regulations herein.

(*e*) Failing agreement by the National Joint Council to any proposed variation of National Working Rules, and pending any other action that may be adopted under this Agreement, the existing approved Rules shall continue to apply.

Failing Agreement on Working Rule Variation.

(*f*) Any Party or Parties (Employer or Operative) in any Area desiring to initiate a variation under this Agreement shall first submit its proposal or proposals, in writing, to its own appropriate Regional body, which shall consider them and forward them to its appropriate National body, together with its own observations thereon, for the consent or otherwise of such National body to the initiation of the variation, and no proposal or proposals shall be communicated to any other Party to this Agreement unless and until such National consent is first had and obtained.

Variations Consent to Initiate. How Obtained.

Any Party or Parties (Employer or Operative) in any Region desiring to initiate a variation under this Agreement shall first submit its proposal or proposals, in writing, to its appropriate National body for its consent to initiate the variation or otherwise, and no proposal or proposals shall be communicated to any other Party to this Agreement unless and until such National consent is first had and obtained.

(*g*) Any Variation Amendment made by the Council shall continue in force until further amended by the Council in accordance with the Rules and Regulations herein and shall apply to all grades and

Duration and Application of Variation Amendments.

all sections of the Industry similarly, unless otherwise provided for in these Rules or expressly decided by the Council.

Procedure in the Case of Deadlock.

13. After the procedure for arriving at a decision on any matter before the Council has been carried out in accordance with this Constitution or in accordance with the National Emergency Disputes procedure incorporated by reference in Rule 9 (*b*) thereof without a settlement having resulted therefrom:—

(*a*) It shall be the duty of the Council to appoint a Special Committee to examine the position with a view to ascertaining upon what terms the question at issue might be settled. The committee shall have full power of conference with the executives of the Adherent Bodies and shall report to the Council within one month from the date of appointment.

(*b*) Failing settlement by the means described in 13 (*a*) above, it shall be the duty of the Council to refer the matter to arbitration. The method of arbitration shall be determined in each case by a majority of the Council present and voting.

No Stoppage of Work.

14. Pending the completion of the procedure set out in the foregoing Rules, no stoppage of work shall take place on any pretext whatever.

Affiliation to Council. Applications for.

15. Any national body desiring to become affiliated to this Council shall make application in writing to the Joint Secretaries, who shall cause the matter to be laid before the Council, which, before deciding thereon, shall invite the observations of the then Parties hereto and shall then consider and deal with the application.

Parties Desiring to Retire.

16. Any Party desiring to retire from this Agreement may do so on giving notice in writing on or before the 1st January in any year, to expire at the Annual Meeting, but shall remain liable for any undischarged share of the expenses due from it in respect of the maintenance of the Council. In such a case the other Parties to the Agreement shall be entitled similarly to give notice within a further 14 days.

All such notices shall formally be reported to the Council at its Annual Meeting and entered upon the Minutes.

REGULATIONS

Governing the Procedure in regard to matters to be submitted to the Council or any Committee thereof.

1. The matter or matters to be submitted shall be definitely and specifically drawn up by the Secretary of the Party concerned, so as to enable the Council or Committee to consider, and if possible to give a decision upon, the precise matters submitted to it. The case to be stated and the evidence taken shall be scrupulously confined to the matter or matters so set forth. *Matters submitted.*

2. The proceedings at a submission to the Council, or to any Committee thereof, shall commence with a short statement by a representative of the appellants (or Parties intervening), in support of which not more than two witnesses may be heard, except by resolution of the Council or Committee. Representatives of other Parties shall then be entitled similarly to make short statements and to call not more than two witnesses. *Evidence and witnesses.*

In every instance, whether before the Council or any Committee thereof, unless by resolution, no representative stating a case shall exceed 15 minutes and no witness shall exceed 5 minutes.

In every instance the representative who opened the case shall have the right of reply but shall not exceed 5 minutes in replying. All witnesses shall be subject to cross-examination.

Direct evidence only admitted.

3. Witnesses and representatives shall give evidence only on matters which are within their personal knowledge, and hearsay evidence shall not be admitted. Where the Council (or any of its Committees) is satisfied, upon representations being made to it, that additional evidence, having a substantial bearing on the case at issue, could be submitted by a witness or representative who, through illness or other sufficient cause, is prevented from attending the appropriate hearing, the Council (or any of its Committees) may make such special arrangements as they consider necessary in order that no delay in its decisions may be occasioned, and that in arriving at its decisions it may be able to take into account such additional evidence.

Parties must be present.

4. All evidence and information in relation to the matter under consideration communicated by one side shall be given in the presence of the other unless representatives or witnesses of the one side have failed to appear after due and proper notice has been given, in which case the hearing shall proceed or such other arrangements shall be made as the Council (or its Committee concerned) shall in its discretion decide.

Evidence completed.

5. All the evidence to be submitted by all Parties concerned and appearing shall be heard before the case is closed.

Witnesses retire.

6. When the case has been formally closed, the

Parties, witnesses and representatives shall retire, and no further evidence shall be heard or information communicated except by request of the Council and/or Committee.

7. If a Member of the Council and/or Committee has represented one of the Parties as a witness or representative or has given evidence or adjudicated upon the case in a lower court, he shall not take part in the proceedings of the Council and/or Committee in regard to that case except as a witness or representative.

Members of Council if witnesses.

8. Regional Joint Committees serve as connecting links between the Council and the localities, and shall comply with the following regulations without variation:

Regional Joint Committees.

(*a*) The total membership of the Regional Joint Committee shall not exceed thirty—viz., fifteen Employers and fifteen Operatives; provided always that only representatives of organisations directly affiliated to the Council shall be eligible.

(*b*) Representation of the Industry on the Operatives' side shall comprise not less than one representative from each Operatives' Trade Association which is directly adherent to the Council, the balance of the representation on the Operatives' side to be allotted on an industrial basis by the National Federation of Building Trades Operatives.

(*c*) Representation on the Employers' side shall be agreed upon between the Parties concerned in each Region, that is, between the Employer bodies who through their National Associations are adherent to the Council.

Should the Parties in any Region fail to agree as to the proper representation of the various Employer bodies, or any of them, the matter shall be referred to a Special Committee appointed by, and representative of, the Employer bodies adherent to the Council, who shall take evidence and give a decision. In assessing the merits of any claim the Special Committee shall regard as relevant the representation on the Council of any body concerned.

Regional Conciliation Panels and Regional Sub-Committees.

9. For the purpose of dealing regionally with differences or disputes referred to the National Joint Council machinery under Rule 9 (*b*) (ii) hereof, each Regional Joint Committee shall appoint a Standing Conciliation Panel, empowered to act in hearing cases and giving decisions in the manner prescribed in Rule 9 (*c*) of the foregoing. For the purposes of dealing with applications for differential margins, or other matters, a Regional Joint Committee may, at its discretion, appoint Sub-Committees which may hear evidence and submit reports to the Regional Joint Committee. Such reports shall, however, have no effect except as assisting the Regional Joint Committee to arrive at whatever recommendations, if any, it thinks fit.

Area Joint Committees.

10. Area Joint Committees may be appointed by the Regional Joint Committees, who will, in that case, define in detail the representation and functions thereof, which shall be consistent with those relating to the Regional Joint Committees. Such Area Joint Committees shall serve as connecting links between the Regional Joint Committee and the individual members in so far as the application of the Working Rule is concerned, and be responsible for the carrying out of the Working Rule Agreement applicable in their respective Areas and for dealing with proposals for Variation Amendments as provided by Regulation 11.

11. (*a*) Where the Regional Joint Committee decide to deal as a regional unit with Variation Amendments, in respect either of the whole Region or of individual districts within the Region, as provided in Rule 12 (*b*) and Rule 12 (*d*) of the Rules of the Council, proposals for such variations shall be initiated regionally, and, if approved by the Regional Joint Committee, shall be submitted to the National Joint Council for approval. Any party to the case in the Region shall have the right of appeal from such a recommendation. If the proposal should fail to secure approval in whole or in part by the Council, it may be dealt with as the Council may determine.

Variation Amendments.

Initiation of, and subsequent procedure.

Regional Initiation.

If any such Variation Amendment initiated at a Regional Joint Committee by any Party or Parties to this Agreement fails to secure agreement there, the initiating Party or Parties shall have the right of appeal to the National Joint Council.

In any event any Party to this Agreement in any other Region, objecting thereto, shall be entitled to intervene and be heard before the National Joint Council and have its objection considered.

(*b*) Where it is arranged that proposals for such Variation Amendments be dealt with as Area units by Area Joint Committees, the following procedure shall apply:

Area Initiation.

(i) If any Variation Amendment initiated at an Area Joint Committee by any Party or Parties to this Agreement secures joint approval at the Area Joint Committee it shall be sent forward to the Regional Joint Committee as a recommended variation. Any Party to the case in the Area shall have the right of appeal to the Regional Joint Committee from such recommendation.

(ii) If any Variation Amendment fails to secure agreement at an Area Joint Committee, then the initiating Party or Parties shall have the right of appeal to the Regional Joint Committee.

In either event any Party to this Agreement in any other Area within the Region concerned, objecting thereto, shall be entitled to intervene and be heard before the Regional Joint Committee and have its objection considered.

If any Variation Amendment secures agreement on appeal or report to the Regional Joint Committee, it shall be sent forward to the National Joint Council as a recommended variation, and shall be dealt with as provided in the first paragraph of section (*a*) above.

If any Variation Amendment as in (i) fails to secure agreement or is disapproved by the Regional Joint Committee, the Area Joint Committee or the initiating Party or Parties shall have right of appeal to the National Joint Council.

If any Variation Amendment as in (ii) fails to secure agreement on appeal to the Regional Joint Committee or is disapproved by that body, the initiating Party or Parties shall have right of appeal to the National Joint Council.

In any of these events, any Party to this Agreement in any other Region, objecting thereto, shall be entitled to intervene and be heard before the appropriate Standing Committee of the National Joint Council and have its objection considered.

(*c*) Variation Amendment recommendations and appeals shall be reported to, and considered by, the Ordinary Meeting of the Council in July, and decisions thereon will normally take effect from the beginning of the pay-week next following October 1st. Decisions by the National Joint Council shall be final, but the fact that a proposal for variation has failed to secure approval shall not debar it from being re-initiated by complying with the regulations as to initiation.

(*d*) All notices respecting Variation Amendments after receiving approval as required by Rule 12 (*f*) of the Rules of the Council, shall be delivered during the first 17 days of February by the Regional Secretary of the initiating Party to the Regional Joint Committee Secretary representing the other side, which shall have 14 days within which to enter counter-notices. Where necessary, the Procedure Committee of the National Joint Council may be consulted as to the regularity or otherwise of proposals intended for submission as Variation Amendments, prior to their submission but after such proposals have received the consent of the appropriate National body as required by Rule 12 (*f*). Particulars of such proposed Variation Amendments recommended by Regional Joint Committees, also notice of appeals (if any), must be sent to the Clerk to the Council on or before 17th April.

Notices re Variation Amendments.

The Procedure Committee shall consider all such Variation Amendment recommendations and appeals and shall determine whether the proposals are in order as Variation Amendments. The decision of the Procedure Committee thereon shall be final and binding. All joint recommendations and appeals must state clearly and specifically the districts covered, and the section or sections covered, and the precise nature of the amendment proposed, failing which the recommendations or appeals may be dealt with in such manner as the Council or its appropriate Committee may consider desirable.

Written evidence required.

(*e*) (i) Upon receipt (as prescribed in section (*d*) above) of particulars of Variation Amendment proposals recommended by Regional Joint Committees and/or notices of appeal, the Clerk shall send to Joint Secretaries of the National Joint Council and of every Regional Joint Committee, not later than the 1st May, a complete list of such particulars and notices received. Any Party in any other Region, desiring to intervene, shall forward to the Clerk, with copy thereof to the appropriate National body, by not later than the 14th May, notification of such desire and a brief written statement of the grounds of its objection.

(ii) In the case of an appeal or a Regional Joint recommendation in respect of a proposal relating to a differential margin, the appropriate Parties in the Region concerned shall forward to the Clerk, no later than the appropriate dates set out in sub-section (iv) hereof, brief written statements adducing reason why, in the district concerned, the section of the Industry specified in the application should (or should not) have the differential margin referred to therein.

(iii) In the case of an appeal or a Regional recommendation in respect of any other Variation Amendment proposal the appropriate Parties in the Region concerned shall forward to the Clerk, not later than the appropriate dates set out in sub-section (iv) hereof, brief written statements specifying the grounds upon which the appeal, recommendation or objection is based, for the use of the appropriate Standing Committee of the Council.

(iv) "The appropriate Parties" and the "appropriate dates" referred to in sub-section (ii) and (iii) above shall be understood to have the following meaning:

	Appropriate Parties	Appropriate Dates
In the case of an appeal.	Appellants.	7th May.
	Respondents directly concerned.	14th May.
In the case of Regional Joint recommendations.	The Initiating Party.	14th May.

(v) The procedure relating to the submission of written evidence for Regional and Area hearings shall be determined by the Regional Joint Committee, but shall be consistent with the provisions of this Regulation.

12. It shall be competent for a duly appointed representative or official of the Regional Joint Committee concerned to be present and participate in any proceedings in an Area connected with an application for a variation Amendment; also for a duly appointed representative or official of the National body or bodies concerned to be present and participate in any such proceedings in an Area or a Region. Such representatives or officials, however, shall have no vote. *(Negotiations in Regions or Areas.)*

NOTE. The N.J.C. Rules are now slightly altered from those printed above. The changes, which were still to be formally published when this book went to print, relate mainly to the Sliding Scale Agreement ending and alterations in the labourer's differential and are dealt with fully in Chapter 9.

APPENDIX 3

ADDRESSES OF THE HON. JOINT SECRETARIES OF THE REGIONAL COUNCILS OF THE NJCBI AND THEIR AREAS OF JURISDICTION

AREAS COVERED BY REGIONS ESTABLISHED UNDER THE NATIONAL JOINT COUNCIL FOR THE BUILDING INDUSTRY AND ADDRESSES of REGIONAL JOINT SECRETARIES

LONDON REGION

Employers' Secretary	*Operatives' Secretary*
47 Bedford Square,	428B Southcroft Road,
London, W.C.1.	Streatham, S.W.16.

Area covered: 15 miles radius from Charing Cross.

SOUTHERN COUNTIES REGION

Employers' Secretary	*Operatives' Secretary*
Sterling Buildings,	77 Portsmouth Road,
Carfax,	Guildford,
Horsham, Sussex.	Surrey.

Area covered: The counties of Oxfordshire, Buckinghamshire, Berkshire, Surrey,* Sussex, Kent,* Hampshire (including the Isle of Wight) and Poole, Swanage and Wimborne in Dorset.

*Excluding London Area.

SOUTH WESTERN REGION

Employers' Secretary	*Operatives' Secretary*
22 Richmond Hill,	Kingsley Hall,
Clifton,	Old Market Street,
Bristol 8.	Bristol 2.

Area covered: The counties of Cornwall (including Scilly Isles), Devonshire, Dorset, Somerset, Wiltshire, Gloucestershire, and Herefordshire.

EASTERN COUNTIES REGION

Employers' Secretary	*Operatives' Secretary*
95 Tenison Road,	3rd Floor, Essex House,
Cambridge.	67–73 Regent Street,
	Cambridge.

Area covered: Norfolk, Suffolk, Cambridgeshire (with Isle of Ely), Bedfordshire, Essex, and Hertfordshire (excluding the London area), Huntingdonshire, and the Soke of Peterborough.

MIDLANDS REGION

Employers' Secretary
36 Calthorpe Road,
Edgbaston, Birmingham 15.

Operatives' Secretary
13 Queens Road,
Coventry.

Area covered: Derbyshire (excluding the Rural District of Chapel-en-le-Frith, the Municipal Boroughs of Buxton and Glossop and the Urban District of New Mills); Leicestershire; Lincolnshire (except the Rural District areas of Grimsby (part), Glanford Brigg and Isle of Axholme, the Urban District of Brigg; the County Borough of Grimsby, and the Municipal Boroughs of Cleethorpes and Scunthorpe); Northamptonshire (except Soke of Peterborough); Nottinghamshire; Rutland; Shropshire (excluding part of the Rural District areas of Oswestry, Ellesmere, Wem and Drayton); Staffordshire; Warwickshire and Worcestershire.

SOUTH WALES REGION

Employers' Secretary
12 Cathedral Road,
Cardiff.

Operatives' Secretary
Transport House,
42 Charles Street,
Cardiff.

Area covered: Glamorganshire, Brecknockshire, Radnorshire, Carmarthenshire, Pembrokeshire, Cardiganshire, and Monmouthshire.

YORKSHIRE REGION

Employers' Secretary
West Bar Chambers,
38 Boar Lane,
Leeds 1.

Operatives' Secretary
2 Hillary Place,
Woodhouse Lane,
Leeds 2.

Area covered: East and West Ridings of Yorkshire (except Sedbergh), the City of York, the part of the North Riding not covered by the Northern Counties Regional Joint Committee, Worksop and part of the Rural District of East Retford in Nottinghamshire, and part of Lincolnshire (i.e. the County Borough of Grimsby, the Urban Districts of Scunthorpe and Frodingham, Winterton, Barton-on-Humber, Brigg & Cleethorpes, the Rural Districts of the Isle of Axholme and Glanford Brigg, and part of the Rural Districts of Grimsby, Caistor and Louth).

NORTH WESTERN REGION

Employers' Secretary
20 St. Mary's Parsonage,
Manchester 3.

Operatives' Secretary
Spinners Hall,
2 Ashton Road East,
Failsworth, Manchester.

Area covered: The counties of Lancashire and Cheshire (except Liverpool, Birkenhead and the Wirral Peninsula), Cumberland,

Westmorland, Anglesey, Caernarvonshire, Denbighshire,
Flintshire, Merionethshire and Montgomeryshire; the
district of Sedbergh in Yorkshire; the North Eastern portion
of Derbyshire, including Glossop, New Mills, Buxton, the
Rural Districts of Glossopdale, Hayfield and Chapel-en-le-
Frith and the part of the Bakewell Rural District north of
the Dore and Chinley railway line; part of Northern
Shropshire, including Oswestry, Ellesmere, Market Drayton,
Wem and Whitchurch.

NORTHERN COUNTIES REGION

Employers' Secretary
15 Norfolk Street,
Sunderland.

Operatives' Secretary
17/18 Emerson Buildings,
Blackett Street,
Newcastle upon Tyne.

Area covered: The counties of Northumberland, Durham and that part of
the North Riding of Yorkshire north of a line running along
the southern boundaries of the Reeth, Richmond, Bedale,
Thirsk and Stokesley Rural Districts, and including (in the
Northern Region) the Civil Parishes of Westerdale, Danby,
Glaisdale and Newton Mulgrave in the Whitby R.D.,
Loftus U.D., and all areas in Yorkshire to the North of this
line.

SCOTLAND

Employers' Secretary
13 Woodside Crescent,
Glasgow, C.3.

Operatives' Secretary
6 Fitzroy Place,
Glasgow C.3.

LIVERPOOL and DISTRICT

Employers' Secretary
Federation House,
Hope Street,
Liverpool 1.

Operatives' Secretary
22 Falkland Street,
Islington,
Liverpool 3.

Area covered: (a) On the Lancashire side, within a circle having a radius
of 10 miles from the Liverpool Landing Stage, except
where the circle overlaps the Widnes and St. Helens
Boundaries, when the following shall apply:
i. WIDNES BOUNDARY—The boundary of that
portion of the Widnes District running from the
North Bank of the River Mersey to the point at
which it meets the boundary of the St. Helens
District shall be a line outside of and threequarters
of a mile from and running parallel with the Widnes
Borough boundary from the North Bank of the
River Mersey to the Southern end of Greensbridge
Lane, then along Greensbridge Lane to the boundary
of the St. Helens Association.

ii. The St. Helens Area comprises the County Borough of St. Helens and the whole of the following townships or parishes: Whiston, Rainhill, Windle, Eccleston, Bold and the Urban District Council Districts of Prescot, Rainford and Haydock.

(*b*) On the Cheshire side, within a circle having a radius of 10 miles from the Birkenhead Town Hall; the boundary line with the Chester Area being just south of Stanlow Point on the Mersey, Ellesmere Port, Whitby, Capenhurst Station, and Puddington.

PROCEDURE UNDER THE EMERGENCY
DISPUTES AGREEMENT

Prevention of Disputes in the Building Trade

AGREEMENT
between
THE NATIONAL FEDERATION of
BUILDING TRADES EMPLOYERS
and
THE NATIONAL FEDERATION of
BUILDING TRADES OPERATIVES
8TH JULY, 1927[1]

FOREWORD

Machinery such as is provided by the National Joint Council, the Conciliation Board and the Demarcation Committee has long existed for dealing with disputes that may arise from time to time in the Building Industry between the parties thereto. That machinery is not intended to be superseded in any way by the Agreement hereinafter set out.

The specific object of this Agreement is to PREVENT disputes involving loss of time and money to all concerned, and by establishing joint machinery capable of dealing expeditiously and effectively with irregularities and disagreements in their earliest stages, to PREVENT any unnecessary cessation of work.

This Agreement is set out in simple terms, and if administered

[1] Commonly known as the "Green Book Procedure".

in the spirit in which it is conceived, should foster the spirit of confidence and goodwill which is essential to the maintenance of friendly and peaceful relationship in the Industry.

AGREEMENT AND REGULATIONS RELATING TO EMERGENCY DISPUTES

AGREEMENT

1. An agreement, made the 8th day of July, 1927, between the National Federation of Building Trades Employers (hereinafter referred to as the Employers) and the National Federation of Building Trades Operatives and other Operative National Bodies (hereinafter referred to as the Operatives) for dealing with emergency disputes by providing for:

(*a*) Joint official endeavours to prevent stoppages of work, or, if those fail, then for joint official action to obtain a resumption of work pending reference:

(i) to an appropriate Conciliation Board, National Joint Council or Demarcation Committee, hereinafter referred to as "existing machinery for dealing with disputes," if any, or

(ii) to the joint emergency disputes Commissions hereinafter provided.

(*b*) Failing reference as above report to respective National Executives for their appropriate action.

2. The parties hereto being agreed that in the event of any dispute or difference arising between their respective members or any of them, every means for effecting an amicable settlement should be exhausted before resorting to direct action, hereby undertake not to instruct their members to strike or lockout or otherwise to take such action as would involve a cessation of work without complying with all the agreements then in existence between the parties and giving the customary notice to terminate the employment. They further undertake not to give support of any kind to their members or any of them who take any action unauthorised by their respective National Executive Body, and to do all that is possible to prevent any unauthorised action upon any particular work.

3. Therefore it is hereby further agreed that as and from the date hereof, should any dispute or difference arising between the parties hereto or between any member of any of them threaten to cause a stoppage of work such dispute, hereinafter referred to as an emergency dispute, shall be reported forthwith by the parties concerned therein to their respective appropriate local officials, and be immediately dealt with jointly by such officials in the manner provided in the Regulations attached to this Agreement or any subsequent agreed modification thereof.

4. This Agreement and the Regulations referred to may be terminated by six months' notice in writing on either side expiring in any year, but the Regulations may be modified at any time by mutual agreement after one month's notice by either side.

REGULATIONS

PART I

OFFICIAL ACTION

1. Any dispute or difference which threatens to cause an emergency dispute shall be forthwith reported by either or both the parties concerned to their respective appropriate local officials (Employer and Operative), together with full particulars, in triplicate, as to the nature and cause of the dispute or difference, who shall respectively report same to their respective appropriate regional officials, in duplicate, for information and transmission to their respective National officials.

2. Upon receipt of the first before-mentioned report it shall be the duty of such local officials to meet without delay and to co-operate with the object of preventing any stoppage of work:

(i) pending a reference of the matter to the appropriate existing machinery for dealing with disputes, or

(ii) should such machinery not be available, pending a reference to a Regional Joint Emergency Disputes Commission as hereinafter provided, and

(iii) at the same time to keep their respective regional officials and, through the latter, their respective National officials fully informed as to the steps taken by such local officials and the results thereof.

3. Upon receipt of any such report from any of their local officials, it shall be the duty of the respective regional officials (Employer and Operative) to meet without delay and to co-operate in support of the efforts of their respective local officials:

(i) to prevent a stoppage of work,

(ii) to secure a reference of the matter to the appropriate existing machinery for dealing with disputes or, with the concurrence of the National officials, to an appropriate Joint Emergency Disputes Commission, as the circumstances may render necessary,

(iii) at the same time to keep their respective National officials fully informed as to the steps taken and the results thereof.

4. Should the emergency dispute arise as a regional instead of as a local dispute, it shall be the duty of either or both the respective regional officials (Employer and Operative) to take immediate steps similar to those set out in Regulation 2 hereof.

5. In any case it shall be the duty of the respective National officials (Employer and Operative), upon being informed that an emergency dispute is imminent or that such has taken place, to confer together and co-operate in like manner and to the same end as already set out in Regulation 2 hereof.

Should it become apparent to the aforesaid National officials at any stage of the procedure prescribed under Regulations 1 to 5 of Part I hereof inclusive that success is not likely to attend the efforts of the officials to prevent a stoppage of work and/or to secure a reference of the dispute to appropriate existing machinery for dealing therewith, or failing such machinery being available, it shall be their duty to confer with a view of bringing about an immediate reference of the dispute to an appropriate Regional or National Joint Emergency Disputes Commission hereinafter provided, and any joint instructions to that effect which such National officials may issue shall take effect accordingly, anything to the contrary in the aforesaid Regulations notwithstanding.

PART II

REFERENCE TO EMERGENCY JOINT DISPUTES COMMISSIONS

1. Joint Emergency Disputes Commissions shall be of two kinds:

(*a*) Regional,

(*b*) National,

composed respectively of three Employer and three Operative representatives drawn from their respective Regional and National Executive Committees and appointed *Ad Hoc* as occasion may require, together with two officials (one representing the Employers and one the Operatives) as members *ex-officio* (and being Regional or National according to whether the Commission is a Regional or a National one).

2. The duties of Joint Emergency Disputes Commissions shall be:

(i) To hold an enquiry without delay either in the place where the dispute is occurring or about to occur or elsewhere as may be deemed most expedient.

(ii) To take evidence from parties concerned and otherwise inquire into the cause and nature of the dispute.

(iii) To decide whether the dispute is referable to any existing

machinery for the settlement of disputes and, if so, to direct
that it be so referred.

(iv) To make such report and recommendations as the
Commission may think fit to the respective National Executive
Committees as to the settlement of such disputes as are not
referable under (iii).

(v) To give such directions as the Commission may think
fit as to preventing a stoppage of work, or in the event of a
stoppage having taken place, as to providing for a resumption
of work, pending a reference under (iii) aforesaid or the consideration of the report and recommendations of the Commission under (iv) aforesaid by the respective National Executive
Committees in joint conference.

3. Joint Emergency Disputes Commissions are empowered to
regulate their proceedings as they think fit, having regard to the
procedure prescribed for the submission of evidence in the Regulations of the National Joint Council for the Building Industry
and the National Board of Conciliation so far as such procedure
may be applicable.

4. The expenses incurred by Joint Emergency Disputes Commissions shall be borne as to one-half by the Employer Bodies
and as to one-half by the Operative Bodies appointing same.

The Employer and Operative Bodies concerned shall also pay
the expenses of those whom they appoint to serve on any Joint
Emergency Disputes Commission.

PART III

APPROPRIATE ACTION BY NATIONAL EXECUTIVE
COMMITTEES

1. Reports by Joint Emergency Disputes Commissions shall
be laid before the respective National Executive Committees
(Employer and Operative) as soon as practicable after they have

been received and be dealt with promptly in one of the following ways:

(i) The recommendations may be approved, and in that case intimations shall be exchanged between the National Executive Committees intimating that they will give effect thereto.

(ii) The recommendations may be disapproved, wholly or partly, in which case communications shall be exchanged between the National Executive Committees as to the further steps which shall be taken in regard to the dispute.

(iii) Where it appears desirable that a Joint Conference of the National Executive Committees shall be convened for the purpose of more effectively dealing with the recommendations of a Joint Emergency Disputes Commission, it shall be held as soon as possible after receipt of such recommendations.

These Regulations are those referred to in the Agreement of 8th July, 1927, and are subject to modification from time to time as therein provided for.

Bibliography

COLE, G. D. H., *Short History of the British Working Class Movement*, 1947, p. 425.

Department of Scientific and Industrial Research, National Building Study No. 29, *Organization of Building Sites*, 1959, p. 73.

EMMERSON, SIR HAROLD, *Survey of the Problems before the Construction Industries*, 1962, p.7.

FREMANTLE, A. F., *England in the 19th Century*, p. 197.

HIGGINS, G. and JESSOP, N., *Communications in the Building Industry*, the report of a pilot study, 1965, p. 61.

HILTON, W. S., *Foes to Tyranny*, 1963, pp. 217, 234, 258.

KNOOP, D. and JONES, G. P., *The Mediaeval Mason*, pp. 61–62, 244, 328.

MANCHESTER UNITY OF BRICKLAYERS, *Quarterly Report*, 30th December 1899.

MARSH, A. I., *Industrial Relations in Engineering*, 1965, p. 134.

MINISTRY OF LABOUR, *Court of Inquiry into Trade Disputes at the Barbican and Horseferry Road Construction Sites in London*, Cmnd. 3396, September 1967.

MINISTRY OF PUBLIC BUILDING AND WORKS, *Monthly Bulletin of Statistics*, July 1966.

MITCHELL, W. G., *Civil Engineering*, Financial Times Survey, 1962.

NATIONAL FEDERATION OF BUILDING TRADE EMPLOYERS, *Statement of Evidence to the Royal Commission on Trade Unions and Employers' Organizations*, par. 52.

NORTH WESTERN FEDERATION OF BUILDING TRADE EMPLOYERS, *A Short History*.

OPERATIVE STONEMASONS' SOCIETY, *Monthly Returns*, 29th April 1858 and 4th July 1872.

POSTGATE, R., *The Builders' History*, 1923, pp. 52, 97, 380.

SALZMAN, L. F., *Building in England*, p. 42.

SHEPHERD, P., *Management in Building*, Report of Proceedings of the Irish National Building Conference in Dublin, 1964.

SNELLING, J. G., A Register of Builders, *Building Technology and Management Journal*, June 1967.

The Builder Journal, Employers Organize, report of meeting in issue of 24th October 1868.

THOROLD ROGERS, J. E., *Six Centuries of Work and Wages*, 1909, p. 543.

WEBB, S. and R., *History of Trades Unionism*, 1911, p. 44.

237

Index

ccidents in construction 192

greements in construction 3

malgamated Slaters, Tilers and
  Roofing Operatives
adherent body to NJC 117
affiliation to NFBTO 58

malgamated Society of Painters and
  Decorators 50
adherent body to NJC 117
affiliation to NFBTO 58

malgamated Society of Woodcutting Machinists
adherent body to NJC 118
affiliation to NFBTO 58

malgamated Society of Woodworkers
adherent body to NJC 117
affiliation to NFBTO 58
and Packing Case Makers 51
foundation of 45
research officer 50
signatory to the CECCB Working
  Rule Agreement 138

malgamated Union of Asphalt
  Workers, affiliation to NFBTO
  58

malgamated Union of Building
  Trade Workers
adherent body to NJC 117
affiliation to NFBTO 58
amalgamation with National
  Society of Street Masons 58
foundation of 45
research officer 50
signatory to the CECCB Working
  Rule Agreement 138
withdraws from NFBTO 70

pprenticeship
the National Joint Apprenticeship
  Board 119
wages payable to apprentices 158

Architects 79

Associated Society of Carpenters
  and Joiners 40
helps to create NFBTO 55

Association of Building Technicians,
  affiliation to NFBTO 58

Bankruptcies in building 27
figures from 1960 to 1965 28
Banwell Committee 189
Barbican building site 182
BATCHELLOR, JOHN 53
Building Advisory Service 94
Building and Monumental Workers
  of Scotland 48
Building firms
and competitive tendering 184
easy capitalization of 184
Building site organization, structural
  outline 16
Building Trades Parliament 113
Building Workers Industrial Union
  44, 53

Cameron Report 182
Casual employment of labour 190
Civil engineering
overtime working 147
value of output 134
Civil Engineering Construction Conciliation Board 4
conciliation machinery 140
foundation of 136
general union representation 6
parties which are signatories to the
  Agreement 138
provision for craft union representation 6
the governing board 135
working rules 141

CLARKE, GEORGE   111
COLE, G. D. H., summarizes reasons
    for 1926 General Strike   47
Combinations Acts   32–33
    punishment of workmen   34
Communications in the building
    industry   11
Construction industry
    annual output   8
    number of firms   9
    pattern of site organization   16
    site labour relations   12
    size of firms   9
Construction site operations   13
Constructional Engineering Union,
    affiliation to NFBTO   58
Contracting, system of   2
COPPOCK, RICHARD   63

Decasualization of labour   25
    report by London School of
        Economics   26
Direct labour employment   2, 74
    by religious and royal masters   76
Document, the   37
    in 1859 London dispute   85
    in London building strike of 1914
        53

Earnings in construction
    and hours in building and civil
        engineering   144
    civil engineering compared with
        building   143
    hourly earnings   152
    in 1408   150
Electrical Trades Union, affiliation
    to NFBTO   58
Elizabethan Act of 1563   31
EMMERSON, SIR HAROLD   5
    comment on division of design and
        production   14
Employers
    in construction, the early years   74
    the Liverpool strike   81

Employment
    diversity of   2
    of operatives according to size c
        firm   10

Federation of Civil Engineerin
    Contractors   136
    signatory to the CECCB Workin
        Rule Agreement   138
FOSTER, THOMAS   114
Friendly Society of Bricklayers
    foundation of   35
    split between Manchester an
        London Orders   40
Fringe benefits   25, 196

General Builders Association   87
General contracting   80
General Strike   46
General Union of Carpenters an
    Joiners, foundation of   35
Green Book Conciliation Procedu
    124
Guaranteed time   172
    new proposals   194

Happy-worker theory   24
HICKS, GEORGE   46
Holidays-with-pay
    administration of holidays   167
    introduced in 1942   166
    the present position   168
Horseferry Road, building site   18

Impressment of labour   75
Incentive schemes
    covered in the National Workin
        Rule   180
    for repairs and maintenance wor
        22
    introduction of the 1947 Agre
        ment   154
    number of men engaged in in
        centives   23

nclement weather, effect on building operations 18

ndustrial Council for the Building Industry 113

ndustrial relations, cost of bad 182

ndustrial Revolution 79

ndustrial Training Board 4

ndustrialized building 179

njury payment 169

abour
  casual employment of 17
  force in construction 3
  officers' role on site 18

abour-only sub-contracting
  and National Working Rule (8) 177
  early growth 50, 77
  Phelps–Brown Committee 178
  their contribution to industry 185

abourers' rates of wages 148

abourers' trade unions 36, 43

iverpool employers in the 1833 strike 81

iverpool Master Builders Association 88
  disaffiliation from NFBTE 90

ondon Master Builders Association, formation of 88

ondon Order of Bricklayers 43
  attitude to Building Workers Industrial Union 53

ondon, the lock-out of 1859 85

Management, development of 11

Manchester Alliance of Painters 40

Manchester Unity of Bricklayers 111

Masons
  impressment of 75
  in the fourteenth century 31

Master craftsmen 75
  become employers of men 78

MITCHELL, W. G. 146

Monasteries, effect of dissolution 77

National Association Building Trades Council 54

National Association of Master Builders 83, 89

National Association of Operative Plasterers 1
  adherent body to NJC 117
  affiliated to NFBTO 58
  amalgamation with Scottish Plasterers Union 51
  foundation of 40

National Board of Conciliation 112

National Building Guild 39

National Economic Development Council 120

National Federation of Building Trades Employers
  administration 100
  early history 92
  foundation of 90
  general meetings 98
  its main objects 96
  signatory to NJC Agreement 118
  signatory to the CECCB Working Rule Agreement 138
  structural outline 95
  total membership 103
  tribute to building unions 52
  working party, structure 106

National Federation of Building Trades Operatives
  affiliation fees payable by unions 59
  an effective federation 53
  and proposals for union amalgamation 51
  appointment of General Secretary 61
  central council 60
  composite section 56, 58
  Demarcation Committee 69
  Exmouth Annual Conference in 1962 71
  fall in membership affiliated 71
  foundation of 45, 55
  regional councils 66
  signatory to the CECCB Working Rule Agreement 138
  structural outline 64
  unions affiliated 58

National Federation of Plumbers and Domestic Engineers, signatory to the NJC Agreement 118

National Federation of Roofing Contractors, signatory to the NJC Agreement 118

National Housebuilders Registration Council 94

National Incomes Commission 133

National Joint Council for the Building Industry 4
and new methods of building 52
conciliation procedure 123
constitution, rules and Regulations 117
growth of its machinery 109
its work on apprenticeship 119
presenting claims 129
structural outline 122

National Society of Street Masons, P. & R., affiliation to NFBTO 58

National Union of Enginemen, Firemen, M. & E. Workers
affiliation to NFBTO 58
signatory to the CECCB Working Rule Agreement 138

National Union of Furniture Trade Operatives, affiliation to NFBT 58

National Union of General & Municipal Workers
adherent body to NJC 118
affiliation to NFBTO 58
signatory to the CECCB Working Rule Agreement 138

National Wages and Conditions Council 115

Navvies' Union 137

Operative Builders Union
challenge to employers 80
end of 39
foundation of 36

Operative Stonemasons Society
Coventry Branch outburst 41
foundation of 35

Organization of building sites 24

Output in construction
per operative 21
various categories 22

OWEN, ROBERT 38

Payment-by-the-hour
in London 86
proposed introduction 84

Pensions and death benefit, proposal for 192

Personnel staff 10

Plumbing Trades Union
adherent body to NJC 117
affiliation to NFBTO 58

POSTGATE, R. 1

Redundancy payments 193

Registration
of builders 187
of operatives 191

Scottish Employers NJC 116

Scottish Plasterers Union
adherent body to NJC 118
affiliation to NFBTO 58

Scottish Slaters, Tilers, R. & C. Workers Society
adherent body to NJC 118
affiliation to NFBTO 58

SHEPHERD, PETER 11

Sickness payments 169

SIDWELL, NORMAN 188

Sliding Scale Agreement in building 45
effect on total wage increase 156
its introduction 115
termination of the agreement 157

SMITH, ADAM, *Wealth of Nations* 33

SNELLING, J. G. 187

SPARKES, MALCOLM 113

Statute of Labourers 30